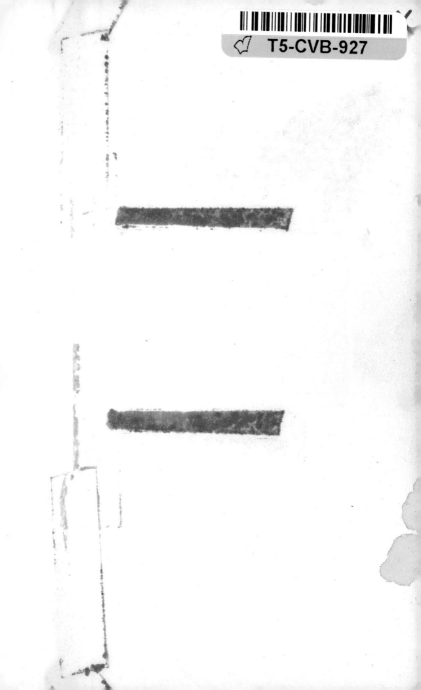

HERALDRY EXPLAINED

HERALDRY
EXPLAINED

by
ARTHUR CHARLES FOX-DAVIES

Introduced by
L. G. Pine

DISCARDED

CHARLES E. TUTTLE COMPANY : PUBLISHERS
Rutland, Vermont

Published by the Charles E. Tuttle Co., Inc.
of Rutland, Vermont and Tokyo, Japan
with editorial offices at
Suido 1-chome, 2-6 Bunkyo-ku, Tokyo, Japan

First published by The Burke Publishing Co. Ltd. 1906
Second edition 1925
First Tuttle edition 1971

Library of Congress Catalog Card No. 78–142780

International Standard Book No. 0-8048-0320-X

Printed in Great Britain

INTRODUCTION

THE simplest explanations are the best, and this applies to the present work in which heraldic usage and terms are very well set out. A bookseller who specialised in heraldic literature used always to recommend *Heraldry Explained*, for the beginner in the subject. Unfortunately the work has long been out of print, and prices of the book secondhand have soared in consequence. The reprint of this excellent little work will be much welcomed, especially with the large increase in heraldic interest.

With regard to one matter only do the words of the author himself need to be repeated, 'in relation to books of ancient date upon the subject of heraldry'; that is in relation to his very condensed account on pages 7-8 of the origins of coat armour. Historical study has shown that the possession of identical coats of arms by families unrelated to each other is in clear contradiction to the concept of an evolution of heraldry under strict royal control. Nor should the reader be quick to accept conclusions from *The Right to Bear Arms*, pages 15 and 21, usually ascribed to Fox-Davies's authorship. This slight blemish apart, no better short guide in English to the art and science of heraldry is likely to be available.

L. G. PINE

CONTENTS

DESCRIPTION OF ILLUSTRATIONS

FIG. 1. — The monumental brass of Sir WILLIAM DE ALDEBURGH at Aldborough, Yorkshire, showing his shield and surcoat, upon which are the arms, "Azure, a fesse argent, between three cross crosslets or."

FIG. 2.—A closed helmet from the seal of WILLIAM, EARL OF ALBEMARLE (d. 1242).

FIG. 3.—The Armorial Bearings of FENTON.—*Arms:* Per pale argent and sable, a cross dovetailed in the first and fourth quarters a fleur de lis and in the second and third a trefoil slipped all counter-changed. *Crest:* on a wreath of the colours, a fleur-de-lis sable in front of two arrows in saltire or, barbed and flighted argent.

FIG. 4.—The Armorial Bearings of HOWATSON.—*Arms:* Sable, two chevronels between as many owls in chief and a wolf's head erased argent in base. *Crest:* On a wreath of his liveries, a dexter hand couped at the wrist, appaumé proper.

FIG. 5. — The Armorial Bearings of LEECH. — *Arms:* Ermine, a rose gules, on a chief indented of the last, three ducal coronets or. *Crest:* on a wreath of the colours, an arm erect proper, grasping a snake vert.

FIG. 6. — The Armorial Bearings of HYDE. — *Arms:* azure, a chevron between three lozenges or. *Crest:* on a wreath of the colours, an eagle with wings expanded sable, beaked and membered or.

FIG. 7.—The Armorial Bearings of HILL.—*Arms:* Azure, on a bend between two leopards' faces or, three sprigs each composed of as many cinquefoils vert, stalked and slipped proper. *Crest :* on a wreath of the colours, two arms in armour embowed proper, each charged with a leopard's face azure, the hands also proper, holding a sprig of three cinquefoils as in the arms.

FIG. 8.—The ROYAL ARMS of H.M. KING EDWARD VII. —*Arms :* Quarterly 1 and 4 gules, three lions passant guardant in pale or (England), 2 or, a lion rampant within a double tressure flory and counterflory gules (Scotland), 3 azure, a harp or, stringed argent (Ireland). The shield is surrounded by the Garter, which is encircled by the collar of that Order. The helmet is of gold, is affronté, and is guarded by grilles. The mantling is of cloth of gold, lined with ermine. Upon the helmet is set the royal crown, and thereupon the *Crest,* a lion statant guardant or, crowned with the Royal Crown. *Supporters :* (dexter) a lion guardant or, crowned as in the crest, (sinister) a unicorn argent, armed, crined and unguled or, gorged with a coronet composed of crosses patée and fleurs-de-lis, and therefrom a chain reflexed over the back gold, and standing upon a compartment adorned with the Union Badge of the rose, thistle, and shamrock, and bearing the motto, " Dieu et mon droit."

FIG. 9.—The Armorial Bearings of the EARL OF CARYS-FORT, K.P. *Arms :* Quarterly 1 and 4 ermine, on a fesse gules, a lion passant or (Proby), 2 and 3 argent two bars wavy azure, on a chief of the second an estoile between two escallops or (Allen). The escutcheon is surrounded by the circlet and collar of St. Patrick. *Crest :* on a wreath of the colours, an ostrich's head erased proper, ducally gorged or, in the beak a key of the last. *Supporters :* (dexter) an ostrich proper, ducally gorged or, in the beak a key of the last (sinister) a talbot sable.

FIG. 10.—The Armorial Bearings of LAWSON.—*Arms :* Per chevron argent and or, a chevron invected sable, plain cottised vert, between two martlets in chief and a trefoil slipped in base of the fourth. On the escutcheon is the inescutcheon of Ulster, the badge of a Baronet. *Crest :* on a wreath of the colours, between two arms embowed proper, holding a sun in splendour, a trefoil, as in the arms, the whole surmounted by a rainbow also proper.

Fig. 11.—The Armorial Bearings of JERNINGHAM, K.C.M.G.—*Arms :* Quarterly, 1 argent, three lozenge-shaped arming-buckles gules (Jerningham); 2 azure, a fesse dancettée, the two upper points terminating in fleurs-de-lis or (Plowden); 3 gules, on a bend between six cross crosslets fitchée argent, an inescutcheon or, charged with a demi-lion rampant pierced through the mouth by an arrow within a double tressure flory counter-flory of the first, a crescent for difference (Howard); 4 gules, three lions passant guardant in pale or, a label of three points argent (Thomas of Brotherton); 5 gules, a lion rampant argent (Mowbray); 6 quarterly, 1 and 4 France, 2 and 3 England, a bordure argent (Thomas of Woodstock); 7 or, a chevron gules (Stafford); 8 azure, a bend argent, cottised or, between six lions rampant of the last (Bohun); the escutcheon being encircled by the ribbon of the Order of Saint Michael and Saint George. *Crest :* Out of a ducal coronet or, a demi-falcon with wings displayed proper.

Fig. 12.—The heraldic chapeau.

Fig. 13.—The Armorial Bearings of BEWES.—*Arms :* Argent, a lion rampant, tail nowed gules, gorged with an Eastern crown or, in chief three falcons proper belled of the third. *Crest :* on a chapeau gules, turned up ermine, a Pegasus rearing on his hind legs, of a bright bay colour, mane and tail sable, wings displayed or, holding in the mouth a laurel branch proper.

Fig. 14.—The Armorial Bearings of WEST.—*Arms :* Argent, a fesse dancetté sable. *Crest :* out of a ducal coronet or, a griffin's head azure, beaked and eared gold.

Fig. 15.—The Armorial Bearings of CASEMENT.—*Arms :* Ermine, a lion rampant guardant proper, charged with a mullet gules, and holding in the paws a sword erect also proper, pommel and hilt gold, encircled round the point with a wreath vert, on a chief embattled gules, a tower argent, between two elephants' heads erased or. *Crest :*

a mural crown gules, issuing therefrom a demi-tiger rampant guardant proper, charged with a mullet of the first and crowned with an Eastern crown or, holding in the paws a sword erect proper, pommel and hilt gold, the point encircled by a wreath vert.

Fig. 16.—The Armorial Bearings of FARQUHAR, K.C.B. —*Arms :* Or, a lion rampant sable, supporting a sword erect proper, the blade encircled by a wreath of laurel also proper, between three sinister hands couped gules, a chief wavy azure, thereon out of waves of the sea a representation of a fortified town of the third, and above the word "Gluckstadt" in letters of gold, the escutcheon being surrounded by the ribbon of the Order of the Bath. *Crest :* out of a naval crown or, a sword as in the arms, and a flag flowing towards the sinister in saltire azure, inscribed with the word "Acheron" in letters of gold, surmounted by a dexter hand issuant gules.

Fig. 17.—The Armorial Bearings of CALDWELL.—*Arms :* Or, three piles sable, each charged with a fountain; in base four barrulets wavy alternately gules and vert. *Crest :* Out of an Eastern crown argent, the rim inscribed "Gooty" in letters sable, a demi-lion rampant holding in its dexter paw a falchion proper, and supporting in its sinister paw an escutcheon azure charged with a representation of the medal conferred upon Sir Alexander Caldwell in commemoration of his services at the siege of Seringapatam pendent from a riband tenné.

Fig. 18.—The Armorial Bearings of SEALE.—*Arms :* Or, two barrulets azure, between three wolves' heads erased sable, in the fesse point a mural crown gules; the escutcheon charged with his badge of Ulster as a Baronet. *Crest :* Out of a crown vallery or, a wolf's head argent, the neck encircled with a wreath of oak vert.

Fig. 19.—The Armorial Bearings of the Royal Borough of KENSINGTON.—*Arms :* Quarterly gules and or, a celestial crown in chief and a fleur-de-lis in base of the last, in the dexter canton a mullet argent, in the first quarter; a cross flory between four martlets sable in the second; a cross botonny gules, between four roses of the last, stalked and leaved proper in the third; a mitre of the second in the fourth; all within a bordure quarterly or and sable.

Fig. 20.—Helmet and crest of THOMAS, EARL OF LANCASTER (from his seal, 1301).

Fig. 21.—Helmet and crest of WILLIAM DE MONTAGU, Earl of Salisbury; d. 1344 (from his seal).

Fig. 22.—Armorial Bearings of SUTHERLAND, G.C.M.G. *Arms :* Or, a fesse wavy azure, issuant therefrom a sun in splendour or, between two mullets in chief and a fleur-de-lis in base of the second, the escutcheon being surrounded by the ribbon and the collar, and pendent the badge of a G.C.M.G. *Crest :* A cat saliant, holding in the mouth a thistle leaved and slipped proper, between two roses gules, leaved and stalked vert. *Supporters :* Dexter, a sailor habited, holding in the exterior hand a coil of rope, suspended therefrom a sinker of a sounding machine all proper; sinister, a Lascar seaman habited, holding in the exterior hand a flagstaff proper, therefrom flowing to the sinister a banner azure, charged with a rudder in bend sinister surmounted by an anchor or.

Fig. 23.—Armorial Bearings of LORD NEWLANDS.—*Arms :* Vair, on a chevron gules, three bezants, a chief gyronny of eight or and sable. The escutcheon is charged with his badge of Ulster as a Baronet; upon a wreath of his liveries is set for *Crest* a bloodhound sejant proper, and on an escroll over the same this *Motto*, " Aye ready." *Supporters :* On either side, a dapple-grey horse, gorged with a riband, and suspended therefrom an escutcheon gules charged with three bezants in chevron.

Fig. 24.—Armorial Bearings of SWINTON of that Ilk. —*Arms :* Sable, a chevron or, between three boars' heads erased argent. *Crest :* On a wreath of his liveries, a boar chained to a tree proper. *Supporters :* (personal to head of the family)—Two boars rampant sable, armed, crined, and unguled or, langued gules.

Fig. 25.—Armorial Bearings of CLUNY MACPHERSON. *Arms :* Per fesse or and azure, a lymphad of the first, with her sails furled, oars in action, mast and tackling all proper, flags flying gules, in the dexter chief point a hand couped grasping a dagger point upwards gules, in the sinister chief a cross crosslet fitchée of the last. Upon a wreath of his liveries is set for *Crest*, a cat sejant proper. *Supporters :* Two Highlanders in short tartan jackets and hose, with steel helmets on their heads, thighs bare, their shirts tied between them, and round targets on their arms.

Fig. 26.—Armorial Bearings of Earl of Shrewsbury, Waterford, and Talbot. *Arms :* Quarterly, 1 and 4 gules, a lion rampant within a bordure engrailed or (Talbot); 2 and 3 azure, a chevron between three mullets or (Chetwynd), and impaling the arms of Palmer-Morewood, namely, quarterly 1 and 4 vert, a tree eradicated argent, in the dexter chief point a trefoil of the last (Morewood); 2 and 3 argent, two bars sable, the upper charged with two and the lower with one trefoil slipped of the field, in chief a greyhound courant of the second, collared or (Palmer) and in pale behind the escutcheon is placed the white wand appertaining to the office of Great Seneschal of Ireland. *Crests :* 1. on a chapeau gules, turned up ermine, a lion statant, tail extended or (Talbot); 2. upon a wreath of the colours, a goat's head erased argent, attired or (Chetwynd). *Supporters :* On either side of the escutcheon a talbot argent.

Fig. 27.—The Standard of the Earl of Northumberland (d. 1527) showing his badges.

Fig. 28.—The badge of William de la Pole, Duke of Suffolk. An ape-clog argent, the chain or.

Fig. 29.—A badge of King Edward IV. The "rose-en-soleil," being a combination of the two badges of the white rose and the blazing sun.

Fig. 30. The Armorial Bearings of Ross. *Arms :* Gules, three estoiles in chevron between as many lions rampant argent ; and for an honourable augmentation, a chief or, thereon a portion of the terrestrial globe proper, the true meridian described thereon by a line passing from north to south sable, with the Arctic circle azure, within the place

of the magnetic pole in latitude 70° 5' 17" and longitude
96° 46' 45" west, designated by an inescutcheon gules,
charged with a lion passant guardant of the first; the
magnetic meridian shown by a line of the fourth passing
through the inescutcheon with a correspondent circle,
also gules, to denote more particularly the said place
of the magnetic pole; the words following inscribed on
the chief, viz., "Arctæos Numine Fines." *Crests :* 1. on a
wreath of the colours, on a rock a flagstaff erect, thereon
hoisted the Union Jack, inscribed with the date June 1,
1831 (being that of discovering the place of the magnetic
pole), and at foot, and on the sinister side of the flagstaff,
the dipping needle, showing its almost vertical position, all
proper; 2. on a wreath of the colours, a fox's head erased
proper.

Fig. 31.—Armorial Bearings of LANE of King's Bromley.
—*Arms :* Party per fesse or and azure, a chevron gules
between three mullets counterchanged of the field, a canton
of the arms of England, namely gules, three lions passant
guardant in pale or. *Crest :* upon a wreath of the colours,
a strawberry-roan horse saliant, couped at the flanks,
bridled sable, bitted and garnished or, supporting between
the feet an imperial crown proper.

Fig. 32.—The Coronet of a Duke.

Fig. 33.—The Coronet of a Marquess.

Fig. 34.—The Coronet of an Earl.

Fig. 35.—The Coronet of a Viscount.

Fig. 36.—The Coronet of a Baron.

Fig. 37.—The Royal Crown.

Fig. 38.—The Coronet of the Prince of Wales.

Fig. 39.—The Coronet of younger sons of the Sovereign.

Fig. 40.—A Bookplate designed by "C. Helard,"
showing the Arms of Crozier, viz. "Or, on a cross between
four fleurs-de-lis azure, a crozier of the field. *Crest :* on a
wreath of the colours, a demi-eagle displayed proper,
charged on the breast with a cross patée or."

Saracen's head couped proper, wreathed round the temples argent and sable (Westhead); 2. on a wreath of the colours, a demi-eagle displayed with two heads azure, charged on the breast with the fasces, swords and chaplet as in the arms (Brown).

FIG. 55.—Armorial Bearings of COCHRAN-PATRICK.— *Arms:* Quarterly 1 and 4, counterquartered i. and iiii. argent, a saltire sable between a cinquefoil in chief and a crescent in base gules, and on either side an eagle's head erased azure, on a chief engrailed of the second, three roses of the field (Patrick), ii. and iii. argent, on a chevron gules, between three boars' heads erased azure, a mullet or (Cochran); 2 argent, on a chevron gules, between three cross crosslets fitchée sable, a spur-revel between two lions counterpassant or within a bordure of the second (Kennedy of Underwood); 3 or, three hunting-horns vert, garnished and stringed gules (Hunter of Hunterston). *Crests:* 1. on a wreath of the liveries, a hand proper, holding a saltire sable (Patrick); 2. on a wreath of the liveries, a horse trotting sable, crined and unguled or (Cochran).

FIG. 56.—The English "difference-marks"—(*a*) label, (*b*) crescent, (*c*) mullet, (*d*) martlet, (*e*) annulet, (*f*) fleur-de-lis, (*g*) rose, (*h*) cross moline, (*i*) double quatrefoil.

FIG. 57.—Armorial Bearings of DARBISHIRE.—*Arms:* Quarterly, 1 and 4 gules, on a pile issuant from the dexter canton argent, three leopards' faces of the field (Darbishire); 2 and 3 argent, a cross pointed and voided sable (Dukinfield), a crescent on a crescent for difference. *Crest:* On a wreath of the colours, issuant from clouds, a dexter arm in armour embowed, holding in the hand proper a cross pointed and voided sable.

FIG. 58.—Armorial Bearings of HAIG OF BEMERSYDE. —*Arms:* Azure, a saltire between two mullets in chief and base, and a decrescent and increscent in fesse argent. *Crest:* on a wreath of his liveries a rock proper. *Mantling* gules, double argent.

Fig. 59.—Armorial Bearings of George Ogilvy Haig, being the Arms of Haig of Bemersyde as above, differenced by a bordure sable, charged with three cows' heads caboshed argent.

Fig. 60.—Armorial Bearings of Haig of Pen-Ithon, being the arms of Haig of Bemersyde as above, differenced by a bordure invected or, charged with three talbots' heads erased, alternately with as many crescents gules.

Fig. 61.—Armorial Bearings of F.-M. Lord Haig (as Major-Gen. Douglas Haig) showing the Arms of Haig of Bemersyde, differenced by a bordure parted per pale argent and sable, charged with three cows' heads caboshed, all counterchanged and quartered with the Arms of Veitch.

Fig. 62.—The Arms of Brittany, viz. an ermine shield.

Fig. 63.—Ermine.

Fig. 64.—Ermines.

Fig. 65.—Vair.

Fig. 66.—Potent.

Fig. 67.—The Tincture Lines.

Fig. 68.—Arms of David de Strabolgi, Earl of Athol, " paly or and sable."

Fig. 69. — Armorial Bearings of Nutting. —*Arms :* Chevronny of six gules and vert, three gryphons segreant or, on a chief of the last as many nut-branches slipped proper. *Crest :* On a wreath of the colours, a demi-gryphon segreant enclosed between two nut-branches proper.

Fig. 70.—The Partition Lines.

Fig. 71.—The Armorial Bearings of Lord Beaumont (d. 1396).—*Arms :* Quarterly, 1 and 4 azure, semé-de-lys, a lion rampant or (Beaumont); 2 and 3 azure, three garbs or (Comyn). From his Garter Plate.

Fig. 72.—The Armorial Bearings of Lord De la Warr (d. 1398). Gules, crusuly and a lion rampant argent.

Fig. 73.—Armorial Bearings of Lancaster of King's Lynn. *Arms :* Or, two bars sable, on a pale engrailed

ermine, four cinquefoils paleways of the second.   *Crest :*
On a wreath of the colours, two cinquefoils fesseways,
that on the dexter sable, that on the sinister or, surmounted by a third cinquefoil per pale of the last and first.

FIG. 74.—Armorial Bearings of POOLER.—*Arms :* Per
pale or and argent, a fesse azure, between two lions' heads
erased in chief gules and a crescent in base of the third.
Crest : On a wreath of the colours, a falcon rising proper,
belled or, and charged on the breast with a lozenge gules.

FIG. 75.—Armorial Bearings of SCROPE of Danby.—
Arms : Azure, a bend or.   *Crest :* Out of a ducal coronet
or, a plume of five ostrich feathers proper.

FIG. 76.—Armorial Bearings of BURKE.—*Arms :* Or, a
cross gules, in the dexter canton a lion rampant sable.
Crest : On a wreath of the colours, a cat-a-mountain sejant
guardant proper, collared and chained or.

FIG. 77.—Armorial Bearings of BASTARD.—*Arms :* Or, a
chevron azure.   *Crest :* On a wreath of the colours, a
dexter arm embowed in plate armour proper, garnished or,
the elbow towards the sinister, the hand in a gauntlet
grasping a sword also proper, pommel and hilt gold, in
bend sinister the point downwards.

FIG. 78.—Armorial Bearings of LEGG.—*Arms :* Sable, on
a pile or, between two books argent, clasped and garnished
in base of the second, a leg couped at the thigh in armour
of the field, spurred and garnished gold.   *Crest :* On a
wreath of the colours, a dexter arm in armour sable,
garnished gold, holding in the hand a roll of paper argent,
between roses or.

FIG. 79.—Armorial Bearings of DEWAR.—*Arms :* Or, a
ship in the sea proper, sails furled, streamers flying azure,
on a chief of the last two boars' heads erased argent,
armed gules.   *Crest :* On a wreath of the colours, an
anchor erect sable, cabled gules.

FIG. 80.—Arms of JOHN DE BRETAGNE, EARL OF RICH-
MOND (d. 1334).—Chequy or and azure, a bordure of
England (*i.e.* gules, thereon lions passant gardant or), a
quarter ermine.

Fig. 81.—Armorial Bearings of Tonge.—*Arms :* Azure, on a bend invected plain cotised or, between six martlets of the last, a lion passant between two grappling-irons the flukes upwards of the first. *Crest :* On a wreath of the colours, in front of an arm embowed in armour, the hand proper grasping a grappling-iron in bend sinister sable, a lion sejant of the last pierced in the sinister shoulder with an arrow proper.

Fig. 82.— Armorial Bearings of Carruthers.—*Arms :* Gules, two chevronels engrailed between three fleurs-de-lis or. *Crest :* on a wreath of the liveries, a cherub's head proper.

Fig. 83.— Armorial Bearings of Whittaker.— *Arms :* Sable, three mascles argent. *Crest :* On a wreath of the colours, a cubit-arm erect in armour holding in the hand a sword all proper.

Fig. 84.—Armorial Bearings of Blake, G.C.M.G.—*Arms :* Quarterly, 1 and 4 argent, a fret gules, a crescent for difference (for Blake); 2 and 3 sable, three lions passant between four bendlets argent, in chief a fleur-de-lis of the last for difference (for Browne), the escutcheon being encircled by the ribbon and the collar of the Order of St. Michael and St. George. *Crest :* on a wreath of the colours, a cat-a-mountain passant guardant proper, charged with a crescent gules for difference.

Fig. 85.—Armorial Bearings of Allen-Hoblyn.—*Arms :* Azure, a fesse or, two flaunches ermine. *Crest :* On a wreath of the colours a tower proper (and for distinction on each a cross crosslet or).

Fig. 86.—Armorial Bearings of Rutherfurd.— *Arms :* Argent, an orle, and in chief three martlets gules, all within a bordure ermine. Upon a wreath of his liveries is set for *Crest*, a mermaid holding in her dexter hand a mirror, and in her sinister a comb, all proper.

Fig. 87.— Armorial Bearings of Gladstone. —*Arms :* Argent, a savage's head affrontée, dropping blood, wreathed about the temples with holly proper, within an orle flory gules, all within eight martlets in orle sable. *Crest :* upon a wreath of the colours, issuant from a wreath of holly proper, a demi-griffin sable, supporting between the claws a sword enfiled with a wreath of oak all proper.

Fig. 88.—Armorial Bearings of Cunynghame.—*Arms :* Argent, a shakefork sable, between three fleurs-de-lis azure, one in chief and two in the flanges. On a wreath of his liveries is set for *Crest,* a unicorn argent unguled, maned and armed or, lying on a mount vert.

Fig. 89.—Armorial Bearings of Bates.—*Arms :* Barry of twelve per pale azure and argent, counterchanged, on a chevron or, cotised gules, three pallets of the last, each charged with a fleur-de-lis of the third. *Crest :* On a wreath of the colours, five fleurs-de-lis alternately or and gules, in front of a swan's head couped proper, and charged on the neck with six barrulets azure.

Fig. 90.—A lion rampant.

Fig. 91.—A lion passant.

Fig. 92.—A lion statant.

Fig. 93.—A lion sejant.

Fig. 94.—A lion sejant erect.

Fig. 95.—A lion couchant.

Fig. 96.—A lion dormant.

Fig. 97.—A lion saliant.

Fig. 98.—A lion passant guardant.

Fig. 99.—A lion rampant regardant.

Fig. 100.—Armorial Bearings of Mackenzie of Ballone. —*Arms :* Quarterly, 1 and 4 azure, a stag's head caboshed or ; 2 or, a rock in flames proper ; 3 gules, three human legs conjoined at the thigh, armed garnished and spurred or : all within a bordure indented or. *Crest :* On a wreath of the liveries a mountain in flames proper.

Fig. 101.—Armorial Bearings of Dorman. *Arms :* Argent, two bars azure, over all a lozenge sable, thereon three leopards' faces in pale of the field. *Crest :* on a wreath of the colours upon a rock proper, a lion's paw erased sable, grasping a javelin in bend sinister proper, transfixing a leopard's face argent.

Fig. 102.—A dragon passant with wings displayed.

Fig. 103.—Armorial Bearings of Mansergh. *Arms:* Barry wavy of eight argent and azure, gutté-d'eau, on a bend between six arrows barbed and flighted gules, three fountains proper. *Crest:* On a wreath of the colours, a wyvern sejant and erect gules, gorged with a collar wavy argent, and supporting with the claws an arrow erect gules, barbed and flighted argent.

Fig. 104.—Armorial Bearings of the Burgh of Alloa. *Arms:* Argent, on the waves of the sea, an ancient galley sable in full sail, the sail charged with the arms of the Earls of Mar and Kellie, pennon gules, flag of the field, charged with a pale of the second on a chief vert, in the dexter a garland, the dexter half hops, the sinister barley all or, and in the sinister a golden fleece. *Crest:* on a wreath of the liveries a griffin gules, winged, armed and beaked or, langued azure.

Fig. 105.—A unicorn rampant.

Fig. 106.—An heraldic antelope rampant.

Fig. 107.—A sea-dog rampant.

Fig. 108.—An eagle displayed.

Fig. 109.—Armorial Bearings of Ramsay of Kildalton.— *Arms:* Parted per fesse argent and sable, an eagle displayed beaked gules, charged on the breast with a galley, sails furled all counterchanged. *Crest:* On a wreath of the liveries, a unicorn's head couped argent, armed and crined or.

Fig. 110.—Armorial Bearings of Bailey.—*Arms:* Gules, on a fesse nebuly between four martlets, three in chief, and one in base argent, two roses of the first, barbed and seeded proper. *Crest:* On a wreath of the colours, in front of an anchor in bend sinister proper, a female figure, vested vert, supporting with the dexter hand an escutcheon gules, charged with a martlet argent, and resting the sinister on the stock of the anchor.

Fig. 111.—Armorial Bearings of PATTERSON.—*Arms:* Argent, on a fesse dancetté azure, three fleurs-de-lis of the field, on a canton gules, a lion rampant regardant or. *Crest:* On a wreath of the colours, a pelican in her piety vulning herself proper, gorged with a collar dancetté azure.

Fig. 112.—Armorial Bearings of LANIGAN-O'KEEFE.— *Arms:* Quarterly, 1 azure, a lion rampant argent; 2 gules, a knight in armour on horseback at full speed proper, the horse argent; 3 or, a peacock in his pride proper; 4 vert, three lizards in pale or. *Crest:* Upon an antique crown, a gryphon segreant or, holding in the dexter claw a sword erect argent, pommelled gold.

Fig. 113.—Armorial Bearings of Borough of SWINDON. —*Arms:* Quarterly, per fess nebuly azure and gules, a pile argent, thereon three crescents of the second in the first quarter; three castles, one and two of the third in the second; a mitre or in the third; a winged wheel of the last in the fourth, and a chief also of the third, thereon a locomotive engine proper. *Crest:* On a wreath of the colours, a dexter arm embowed proper, grasping two hammers in saltire or.

Fig. 114.—Armorial Bearings of CROOKES.—*Arms:* Or, on a chevron vert, three prisms proper, between in chief two crosses patée of the second, and in base a radiometer proper. *Crest:* On a wreath of the colours, an elephant quarterly or and vert, charged with two crosses patté counterchanged, resting the dexter forefoot on a prism proper.

HERALDRY EXPLAINED

CHAPTER I

WHAT IS A COAT OF ARMS?

THE attempt to answer the query which stands at the head of the chapter must be qualified by the scope of the present work. In pursuit of an answer, many writers have been tempted into paths of antiquarian research and into strange highways and byways of knowledge, and have reached points to which few will care to follow, save those who have long since mastered the elements of the science, the practice, and the art of heraldry. To readers of that category, an elementary handbook of the character of the present work cannot pretend to be a laboured or intricate guide. I would refer such students to my larger work, *The Art of Heraldry.* But there is a large and increasing class of intelligent inquirers into the science of heraldry, for whose requirements there has as yet been no catering, and it is to that class that the present little guide should appeal. There are many who, without wishing to expend the time or trouble necessary to acquire a detailed knowledge of the intricacies of the science, yet, nevertheless, desire to obtain such a broad general grasp of the subject that they may understand the outlines of the matter, and that their own use of heraldic emblems shall be in accord with the laws of the science. My primary object is to explain the rules of heraldry which are observed at the present time, and I only propose to refer to ancient laws and practice to the extent which is necessary by way of explanation. The painstaking antiquary, who desires to know the heraldry of bygone times, that he may translate the heraldic records of the far distant past, will no doubt realise that as times and peoples change, customs alter, and no circumscribed little handbook can deal adequately with different sets of laws often widely divergent.

A coat of arms, then, is a device or emblem or picture intended to be represented upon a shield in colours, which device shall be of a hereditary character as far as the circumstances of the case shall admit.

Taking that as a definition of a coat of arms, one can and should recognise that the origin of coat armour, as a science, is to be found in the personal devices, banners, coins, etc., of historical personages, the idea of which is traceable to the totems of uncivilised races; but, nevertheless, one is not justified in treating such devices as proper coats of arms, for they lacked the essential hereditary character which has always attached as a primary essential to the true coat of arms.

It is now universally agreed—I know of no real authority who holds to the contrary at the present day—that there was no such thing as a coat of arms (as we now use and understand the term) in existence at the time of the Norman Conquest.

In this connection a word of warning may be taken to heart in relation to books of an ancient date upon the subject of heraldry. For the practice of heraldry at the period when they were written they may be consulted and accepted, but for the past history of the science in earlier periods they should be wholly disregarded. The writers knew less, for they had discovered less, than is known at the present day. Writers upon all subjects become, as time advances, less credulous, more exact, less prone to mystify, and a great deal more honest.

The date and the manner of the origin of heraldry has been a matter of much speculation.

We have the absolute blank at the time of the Norman Conquest, and this date can certainly be extended to the beginning of the twelfth century. In the thirteenth century, not only were actual coats of arms in practically universal use throughout Europe, but, moreover, there had by then sprung up the definite and (as far as the needs of that period required) completed science of heraldry, governed by known and accepted rules. Most of the "terms" of that period, and some of the rules, have come down to us, and are in use at the present day; some terms and some rules were to all intents and purposes universal throughout the then Christian Europe, though, of course, different nationalities have since grafted on to the original foundation laws peculiar to themselves and the necessities of their own development.

The most curious part of the matter is this—that if we except those developments of armory, which are provably by the nature of things of later origin, and take the heraldry of the middle of the thirteenth century as a perfected science when judged by the necessities of that period, then we must admit the absence of evidence of any period in which the evolution of the science can be traced; although we have a period of, roughly, one to two centuries in which that development must have occurred.

During that period we get the Crusades. Some writers definitely assign the origin of the science to the Crusades; but it is probably a more correct position to adopt to admit the probability of its origin elsewhere, whilst apportioning to the influence of the Crusades its rapid and universal development.

There have been three sources of origin put forward for coat armour, viz. the shield, the banner, the tabard, and possibly to these might be added the use of seals.

Fig. 4.

The question is unlikely ever to be exactly determined, for the probabilities are that, granting the origin to lie in the personal device, the application of that device to the opportunities for its use which have been enumerated, must have been pretty much coeval.

It is one of the quaint curiosities of heraldry that whilst a coat of arms must, to qualify itself as such, be depicted or be depictable on a shield, the very name itself is derived from the linen surcoat or tabard which was worn over the armour and upon which garment the device in question was represented.

Of course there were even hereditary titles, and there was nobility of birth long anterior to the existence of coats of arms.

Whether at the time of the evolution of

heraldry there was any intention to that end or not, or whether, as is more probable, the result was the natural consequence of the existing conditions, the fact nevertheless remains that by the force of circumstances, chiefly of a feudal nature, the upper classes who asserted nobility of birth were the land-holders, and as such those upon whom leadership in battle devolved.   Now it was in warfare that the necessity for armorial bearings arose. Whether, as some assert, that necessity called armorial bearings into being, or whether it was an after-matter acting only as a strong impetus to a science and practice in its infancy, it is quite unnecessary to decide or to discuss here at greater length.   But it must be recognised that the necessities of a military camp, composed of many small units each controlled by the feudal

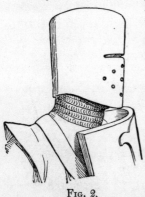

lord from whose lands the unit was recruited, imposed upon the leader of that illiterate unit the use of a pictured standard his followers could muster by. The closed helmet (Fig. 2) which concealed the face, and the armour all of a stereotyped pattern, hid identity so completely that the pictured shield and the embroidered surcoat were

FIG. 2.

foregone necessities in battle.   The closed

helmet was not in use at the time of the Norman Invasion.

Armorial bearings being a necessity of a leader in warfare, and the leaders in warfare being the landowners, such land-holders being the upper class which asserted nobility of birth, the corollary is obvious that armorial devices were the prerogative of the upper class. This prerogative, coat armour, has since, speaking broadly, always remained in all countries.

In early times one could not alienate land to another without the license of the king, consequently it remained the prerogative of the king to sanction the advance of a person to the landowning class. The creation of hereditary rank was also in the hands of the sovereign. But whilst the clever wits of the lawyers evolved the systems of land transfer of which English jurisprudence has successively had cognisance, the prerogatives of the creation of nobility have remained with the sovereign.

Now, I do not assert that the sovereign specifically granted or separately created all the coats of arms we find in use in the thirteenth century. It should be remembered that the power of the sovereign was far from absolute at the period in matters of infinitely greater moment, but in the ordered Rolls of Arms which we find in existence, dating from the closing years of the thirteenth century, it seems to me we have abundant evidence of the attempted control of the arms of his subjects by the heralds and officers of the sovereign.

Since that date there have passed in succession alternating periods of stringent control, of laxity, and of apathy, but the claim to the control has always been there, and the *fons et origo* of the creation of arms has been the prerogative of the sovereign, which embraces the right to call into being nobility of blood and its signs and privileges.

The wording of the most ancient grants of arms which are known, some of which long antedate the College of Arms, makes this apparent, for they are and purport to be grants of nobility, in token of which nobility certain arms are thereby assigned.

Therefore, if we except the very initial years of the evolution of the science of heraldry (and it is by no means provable that they should or need be excepted), one is justified in saying that a coat of arms has always been what it is now, the sign of a nobility of blood dating from the creation of the arms, resting for its authority upon the prerogatives of the Crown, exercised directly or by delegation thereof to its duly appointed officers.

To put the matter in other words, armory is and always has been the prerogative of the privileged class, and armorial bearings are but the outward and visible sign of the *technical* rank of "gentility," the lowest hereditary rank. And so long as the possession of arms is a matter of privilege (even though this privilege is no greater than results from the purchase from the Crown of that technical rank by the payment of the fees upon a grant of arms), so long will a certain (though it may be small) prestige attach to the possession of arms. The world always values anything to which prestige attaches, and the possession of which is in any way a matter of privilege.

The prestige of the possession of arms has of late years considerably increased. The assignment of a coat of arms to a particular person in one of the recognised works of reference on such matters, *e.g.* the Peerage Books, *The Landed Gentry*, Debrett's *House of Commons*, or *Armorial Families*, seldom occurs at the present day without due authority. Of course mistakes are bound to happen, but the day is long past when any arms which might be claimed were admitted without question by the editors of such books. The last-mentioned work has always set up a standard which definitely excludes arms for which official authority cannot be shown.

The result has been noticeably apparent. Not only has the use of unauthorised insignia very greatly declined, but the more extensive usage of heraldic decoration by those who possess arms has been equally in evidence. As a natural consequence, the prestige of heraldry has greatly advanced.

CHAPTER II

HOW TO PROVE A RIGHT TO ARMS

THERE are really, I suspect, but few people whose original interest in heraldry does not emanate from a desire to possess a coat of arms, or to use one. It most frequently happens that in the need of information as to how to use one's own arms on a particular occasion does this interest originate.

I have no copy of Mrs. Glasse's *Cookery Book* by me as I write to verify the quotation, but she is universally credited with having commenced her recipe for the making of hare soup with the very necessary recommendation to " first catch your hare." The advice is no less pertinent in matters of heraldry. It is idle to spend sums of money, which may be large sums, in decorating one's house and belongings with heraldic devices, only to find at a subsequent period that the arms are quite wrong in some detail, or that they belong to a family from which you can prove no descent, or that they never had any legitimate existence at all. Not only may you find that you have wasted a great deal of money, by the necessity of alteration, but you may also find—a discovery which is very annoying if the use of the arms is in such a permanent form that it cannot well be altered — that by setting up a coat of arms you have set up a standing advertisement to all the world of a false pretence of noble or gentle descent, and a notification that you claim a kinship you do not possess, and, to put it briefly, that you have made a foolish exhibition of yourself by using arms to which you have no right.

Let me warn you not to think that because you understand little of such matters yourself others are equally ignorant. The number of people who have a sufficient interest in heraldry to notice a false claim is very considerable. Judging by no more than the letters I have received myself asking whether so-and-so has a right to the arms he uses, the interest in this aspect of the question must be rather widespread. The probabilities are that the interested person will hear nothing himself, but he may rest assured that the point will be discussed often enough by his friends.

Therefore, for reasons of good taste, no less than from motives of economy, I think the very first step that should be taken by any one who proposes to use arms or crest in any form whatever, ought to be to ascertain once and for all—it has only to be done once in a lifetime, as a rule—exactly what his own position may be. Do not rest in confidence on your own opinion of the probity of your father or grandfather—it is quite likely he may have been mistaken—satisfy yourself that you have in your own person a right to arms, which will be recognised by the King's Officers of Arms. Arms to which any less claim is put forward are absolutely valueless. No matter how certain you may feel in your own mind that your right is unquestionable—put it to the test. It may be only that your quarterings are wrongly marshalled; it may be you are using arms without authority whilst a genuine coat belongs to your family all the time; it may be that as a cadet you are using the arms of the head of your house, and that your signs of cadency need to be inserted; it may be only that one impalement should take the place of another. There are all these, and there are other possibilities of going wrong even with a genuine coat of arms. Therefore, put it to the test, and satisfy yourself that you have a right to arms, and satisfy yourself what those arms should be to be correctly borne by yourself. What was perfectly correct for your father, your grandfather, or your uncle, may be quite wrong for you. It may cost you a little money, but believe me that when you have done it, the satisfaction of the definite and certain knowledge you will then possess will leave you pleased you took the necessary steps.

To prove a right to arms in England, it is necessary to show without break male descent from some person to whom arms

(a) have been granted by patent;

(*b*) have been confirmed at one or other of
     the Visitations ;

(*c*) have been officially recorded or registered
     at the College of Arms.

To prove a right to arms in Scotland, it is
necessary to show without break that you are
the heir male (consequently by Scottish law
only *one* person at a time has a right to the
undifferenced arms) of some person to whom
arms

(*a*) have been granted by patent ;

(*b*) have been matriculated upon user, or
     for other reasons, in Lyon Register ;

(*c*) have been matriculated with difference
     as a cadet.

To prove a right to arms in Ireland, it is
necessary to show without break male descent
from some person to whom arms

(*a*) have been granted by patent ;

(*b*) have been confirmed at one or other of
     the Visitations ;

(*c*) have been confirmed by patent ;

(*d*) have been officially recorded or registered
     in Ulster's office.

To prove a right to arms in the Colonies
or elsewhere within the Empire outside the
United Kingdom, it is necessary to show
without break the descent as above specified,
according to whichever of the three countries
may be the country of origin. But, if the
country of origin be foreign and not British,
the right to the arms claimed must be proved

for the original emigrant according to the laws
of his country of origin, and on male descent
shown from the original emigrant the right is
good presumably in his country of origin.   It
will not, however, receive British recognition
until the proofs upon which the foreign right
has been established have been registered in
one or other of the British Offices of Arms.
The fee for such registration is quite trivial,
and the registration is a mere matter of form
if proof by the foreign law is properly in order
and forthcoming.

Descent cannot be presumed, but must be
proved by proper documentary evidence, step
by step and link by link.

If evidence exists sufficient to prove the
descent, I strongly advise that the pedigree
should be officially registered.   Not only does
this safeguard one's right against the future
possibility of the destruction of original evidences, and safeguard against the loss of the
tabulated result of such evidence, but it is important that this should be done on the ground
of economy.   A pedigree of two, three, or four
generations costs but a mere trifling song to put
on record.   If it is left, and it finally becomes
a matter of recording a number of generations,
there is the additional cost of collecting the
evidences and working out the pedigree.   Two
or three generations one knows, and no "working out" can be necessary; beyond that no
one's personal knowledge and recollection

goes, so that the cost mounts up, not in proportion but at a much greater rate. If families would make a point of constantly registering short pedigrees to bring the details up to date every generation, or even every other generation, the cost would be so small that it would never mean a second thought.

Proof should be made and the pedigree registered in whichever Office of Arms may be the original record of the coat of arms to which a right is being established.

Now, there are some writers who deny that the officers of arms have the authority I have indicated, and assert that mere usage can create a right to arms, and that the authority of the Crown is superfluous. Such a standpoint is manifestly absurd, but a discrimination between the two standpoints involves one in a technical discussion quite beyond the scope of the present work. To those who have doubts upon the point, or who desire to fully satisfy themselves, not only as to the validity of the authority of the Crown as presently exercised, but also as to the absence of any other authority or justification for arms, I would recommend a perusal of a small book, *The Right to Bear Arms* (published by Elliot Stock).

CHAPTER III

HOW TO GET A COAT OF ARMS

IF an attempt to prove a right to arms by inheritance has failed—as, unfortunately, such attempts often do fail—or if no claim to arms by inheritance is put forward, and yet in either case a desire exists to obtain a lawful right to use a coat of arms or crest, we next come to the question how can one obtain that right. The answer is simple. There is but one way, and that is by obtaining a formal patent of arms from the Crown.

Patents creating and conferring the right to bear and to transmit armorial bearings to one's posterity are granted by the Crown, through its officers appointed by separate letters patent for the purpose, upon payment of certain fees, the amounts of which have been officially laid down.

There is a certain idea very prevalent that, whereas an ancient coat of arms is most honourable, a modern one is a fit subject for ridicule and contempt, on the sole ground that the latter is supposed to be "purchased."

Arms new and old are on an identical footing; they have all been paid for at some time or another, either in the form of fees and stamp duty upon a grant, or fees upon a registration. The difference in date is the only theoretical difference between an old coat and a new one, and the precedence arising from date is the only advantage the former has over the latter.

If the payment of the fees demanded by the Crown upon the issue of a patent creating a privilege or conferring a benefit or office turn the subject of the grant into a matter of purchase, then a peerage or a baronetage, or a bishopric, are equally matters of purchase, for in each of the above-mentioned cases fees are paid upon the issue of the letters patent by virtue of which they exist.

On payment of the prescribed fees, the Crown will grant arms to any person living as a gentleman in that class of life in which the use of arms is usual.

No man can demand, as a matter of right, that a grant of arms shall be made to him ; but there are few people who desire to have arms and are ready to pay the fees who would meet with the refusal. The reason simply is, that until one is living in the ordinary social position of gentle-people there is never the desire to obtain a grant of arms.

I have never heard of a person with a title, a member of any of the professions, a justice of the peace, or a graduate of a university, being refused a grant of arms, and from the earliest grants of arms, down to the present day, "merchants," under that description and without subterfuge, have continually had grants made to them. But I have been told of specific cases of refusal, and I think the attitude of the Crown and its Officers of Arms is that a grant shall not be made to a person who is notorious for any improper reason, and that a grant shall not ordinarily be made to a retail shopkeeper. But in these days when retailers are knighted and made justices of the peace, it is hard to draw the line, and the practical necessity that the mayor of a big town is under to use arms of some kind, is another reason which is always held to justify a grant.

The procedure relating to a grant of arms in the three countries—England, Scotland, and Ireland—is far from being identical, so we must deal with them separately. The very laws of arms in Scotland differ from those in England. Whilst one cannot but admit that the Scottish practice is theoretically purer heraldry, and more nearly approaches to really ancient observances than does the English, the latter certainly seems much better adapted to the circumstances of the present day.

But as these differences exist, it becomes a matter of some moment to determine under what jurisdiction, English, Scottish, or Irish, one may be. Ordinarily there is no difficulty in coming to a decision. If your male descent is traceable, as far as you know it, or, at any rate, for the last few generations, in the kingdom in which you are presently domiciled, then the jurisdiction to which you must submit is that of the Office of Arms of that kingdom. For an Englishman it will be H.M.'s College of Arms (or the Heralds' College) in Queen Victoria Street, London ; for a Scotsman it will be H.M.'s Lyon Court (or the Lyon Office) in the New Register House, Edinburgh ; for an Irishman, H.M.'s Office of Arms (Ulster's Office) in The Castle, Dublin.

But where the domicile is not in the kingdom in which male descent is traced, there is a certain conflict of opinion. For the purposes of matriculation of ancient arms by a cadet in the Lyon Register, and also for the purposes of matriculation upon user in Lyon Register, and likewise for the purposes of confirmation by Ulster upon ancient user in Ireland, present domicile may properly be entirely disregarded, and resort may be had to Lyon Office or Ulster's Office, as the case may be, by a person resident anywhere within the empire.

But for the purposes of grant pure and simple, where nothing hangs upon descent and ancestry, one is probably safe in depending upon actual domicile and that only. That is the standpoint asserted and acted upon by the College of Arms, which will grant arms to any person being a British subject who is domiciled in England, leaving to Lyon and Ulster Kings of Arms, respectively, the right to grant arms to those of Scottish or Irish domicile. The present Ulster King of Arms, whose patent gives him the control of " Irish Arms," prefers to regard descent rather than domicile ; whilst Lyon King of Arms, whose patent is worded in an entirely different form, I believe holds that he has no alternative but to make a grant to any person in a suitable position of life to use arms who applies to him in due form with a tender of the proper fees, even when domiciled outside Scotland.

Without, however, attempting to decide a matter of controversy, one may with justice leave the matter thus. That where no question of matriculation by reason of Scottish descent is concerned, and where no ground for a confirmation by reason of Irish descent can be alleged, and where it is a matter of grant pure and simple, then one is safe in depending upon domicile and resorting to the official authority of the kingdom in which that domicile exists. With regard to the position of those British subjects resident in the Colonies, and desiring to have arms granted to them, it seems clear that a grant by the College of Arms would have all the necessary validity.

English Jurisdiction

To properly understand the practice in England, it should be stated that at the close

of the fifteenth and the beginning of the sixteenth centuries the control of arms by the
Crown had become very lax, and people had
simply assumed arms very generally, without
troubling to obtain any proper sanction. To
rectify this state of affairs, the sovereign
issued commissions under the Great Seal,
directed to various Officers of Arms, requiring
them in person, or by deputy, to make visitations of the whole of England and examine
the arms in use, deface or rectify those borne
improperly, and record those which were then
properly borne by inheritance. The method
in which these visitations were carried out is
fully explained in *The Right to Bear Arms*,
but the result briefly and broadly was this,
that to every single person, either using arms,
or in a position to use arms throughout England,
three alternatives were presented, viz.

  (*a*) prove the authority for your arms and
        we will register your right to them ;
  (*b*) rectify your arms now ;
  (*c*) " disclaim " in writing that you have any
        right to arms by inheritance.

Three times at least these heraldic visitations passed throughout the country, and it has
since been assumed that genuine arms originat-
ing before that date and properly in use at
that period were then registered. Of course
there may be a few exceptional cases, but to
all intents and purposes that result was accom-
plished. Consequently, in England it is now

impossible to get a "confirmation" of arms
upon user. Either one must prove (in the
manner specified in the previous chapter) that
one possesses a right, or else one does not, in
which case the only way to remedy the matter
is a *grant*. If user is demonstrated for any
appreciable length of time this is often recited
in the patent, and the bare terms of gift and
grant somewhat modified, but the legal fact is
that the patent is really a grant, and the fees
of a grant must be paid upon it. These are
ordinarily in England £76 : 10s.

Application for a grant of arms is made
personally or by letter to one of the Heralds or
Pursuivants of the College of Arms, who will
thereafter act as agent for the applicant who
becomes his client, they being in practically
the same relation as solicitor and client. The
actual formalities are a petition to the Earl
Marshal, who issues his warrant to the Kings of
Arms to make the grant, but those formalities
will be attended to by the Herald or Pursuivant
whom the applicant employs. The fee I have
mentioned covers the whole expense of the
grant.

The design of the arms and crest to be
granted rests with the Kings of Arms. Broadly
speaking, the position is that the applicant makes
a suggestion of his desire in the matter, and
the grant will be of the nearest approach to
his wishes which is consonant with the practice
of the College, the laws of Arms, and the

necessity of sufficient difference in the new grant from any coat which has at any time previously been granted to anybody else.   The design the Kings of Arms propose to grant is submitted to the applicant for his approval before the grant is actually made.

SCOTTISH JURISDICTION

Application in Scotland is made direct to Lyon King of Arms.   The position here is that of dealing with a member of a Government office and a Government official.   In Lyon Office the officials have no personal interest in the fees which are paid.

The cost of a grant of arms made in Lyon Office is £44.   This, of course, is appreciably less than in England ; but whilst an English grant carries to all descendants in the male line, a Scottish grant only conveys a right to the arms to the heir male for the time being, and to the heir of line if a female to bear during life and transmit as a quartering to her issue. Younger sons and other male cadet descendants of the grantee require to rematriculate the arms in Lyon Register in their own names, when due and proper marks of difference to show their position of cadency in the male line of the family are added to the arms.   The cost of a matriculation is £16, and the cadenced version then devolves upon the heir male of the particular cadet who matriculated.   Cadets of that cadet must rematriculate on his version. The changes made for the purpose of cadency never amount to a material alteration.

There were never any visitations in Scotland, and the Register of Scottish Arms is based upon and dates from an Act of the Scottish Parliament in 1672, which required every one to enter his arms within a year and a day. It is well known that this Act of Parliament was not complied with as completely as should have been the case, and consequently the Scottish practice is to matriculate (and not grant) at the ordinary matriculation fees any coat of arms which, by proper evidence, can be shown to have been in use by a proved male ancestor of the applicant at any time before the date of the Act referred to. If the application is made by the heir male, no change is made in the arms; if by a cadet, then only the recognised methods of denoting cadency are employed.

IRISH JURISDICTION

In Ireland application, as in Scotland, is made direct to the King of Arms, in that case "Ulster." As in Lyon Office, so in Ulster's Office, the Officers of Arms have no interest in the fees paid. The fees upon a grant of arms in Ireland amount to £50.

But in Ireland there still exists the unique opportunity of obtaining a "confirmation" of arms upon mere proof of user. The reason for this is that the visitations of Ireland were never carried out to any great extent, and consequently there did not exist that record of arms properly in use in Ireland which resulted in England from the English visitations. In addition to this, the disturbed state of Ireland prevented any real effective control over the native Irish. Consequently successive Ulster Kings of Arms have always been given the power to " confirm " and register arms of which the use can be shown. The present regulation is that user must be proved for at least three generations, and be proved also to have existed for one hundred years. The fees upon a confirmation amount only to £16.

The Limitations of a Grant.

The fees payable upon a grant are £76 : 10s. in England (with a further £15 : 15s. if the limitations extend beyond the applicant's descendants), £50 in Ireland, and £44 in Scotland, and those fees hold good irrespective of the number of persons benefited.

So that unless there is a special reason or desire to restrict the grant to your own descendants, it is short-sighted not to so word the *petition* (the terms of the grant on this point will follow the words of the petition) that the other members of the family come within its compass. Whether the fees are defrayed exclusively by the applicant or collected by him from the members of his family is a matter which is never inquired into and on which the Crown is indifferent.

An English grant can, therefore, be obtained by which the right to the arms granted is conferred upon

(*a*) the grantee and his descendants;

(*b*) as above " and the other descendants of his father ";

(*c*) as next above, and the other descendants of one or more specified brothers of the father of the grantee. This practically amounts to a grant to all the descendants of a grandfather;

(*d*) (if the grantee is a widow) on the grantee as the widow and the descendants of her late husband and the other descendants of her husband's father.

When the petition is so worded, the grant will give permission for the arms to be placed upon a monument to the memory of a deceased husband, father, or uncle, if the grant itself is to their descendants.

A woman may be the petitioner, and it is sometimes possible to rake up a great-aunt, and by making her the petitioner for arms to be granted to herself and the other descendants of her father and of her specified uncles, to bring within the limitations of the grant all the descendants of a great-great-grandfather. Such a case, however, cannot often occur.

A Scottish grant can be extended to the other descendants of a grandfather, but as such a grant does not confer a right to the arms, but only a right to rematriculate them, the question of the limitation is in Scotland of minor importance.

An Irish grant or confirmation can be obtained in the ordinary event to the descendants of a grantee, "and the other descendants of his grandfather." The limitations of an Irish confirmation are entirely at the discretion of Ulster King of Arms. In a case where the user is genuine and straightforward back to a remote period, *e.g.* by an Irish family, of arms which belong to no other family and are peculiar to themselves, from, say, the reign of Queen Elizabeth, Ulster's discretion would probably permit a very wide and extended limitation.

CHAPTER IV

THE COMPONENT PARTS OF A HERALDIC ACHIEVEMENT

ALTHOUGH one usually speaks of a man's heraldic emblems comprehensively by the term of his "coat of arms," this is, however, a term which strictly used only relates to the device which actually figures on the shield. The technical word for the entire device is the "achievement"—a term, however, which is but very seldom met with in actual use.

Ordinarily the heraldic devices of a commoner consist of

(*a*) the arms, *i.e.* the shield and the devices upon it;

(*b*) the helmet;

(*c*) the mantling or lambrequin;

(*d*) the wreath or torse;

(*e*) the crest;

(*f*) the motto.

Such an achievement will be found in Fig. 3, and is similar to what ninety - nine untitled commoners out of a hundred, who have the right to arms, are entitled to bear.

There is an even yet simpler form in which no right exists to a crest, and in which no motto is made use of, but such an achievement must necessarily date from that period anterior to the seventeenth century, when it was possible to possess only a shield of arms or to obtain a grant of arms alone without the grant of a crest. There are, comparatively speaking, but few of such cases which have

survived to the present day, and, as they need
no special rules save this one, that where no
crest legally exists it must needs be omitted
from use and consideration, they can be
dismissed with the remark that it is now
impossible to obtain such a grant, and has
been since the early part of the seventeenth
century. Although arms are an older in-
stitution than the crest, and whilst at one
period the bulk of coats of arms existed
without a crest, yet the estimation placed
upon the crest was so great that crests have
at a subsequent period been granted to
accompany, or have since been registered with
practically all coats of arms which have con-
tinued in existence. Nevertheless, in these
days of modern arms, the position has now
changed, for the mere existence of the right
to a shield of arms without a right to a crest
is proof that the arms must date from before
about 1600, which at the present day is something to be exceedingly proud of.

In addition to the shield, crest, motto,
helmet, torse, and mantling, which at the
present day make up the ordinary coat of arms,
an untitled commoner may also possess

(g) supporters;
(h) a compartment;
(j) a *cri-de-guerre*;
(k) a standard;
(l) a badge;
(m) an augmentation;

whilst a knight, commander, or companion of any order will possess

(*n*) the circle and badge of his order.

A Knight Grand Cross or Knight Grand Commander of any order, or a Knight of the Garter, Thistle, or St. Patrick, will add

(*o*) the collar of his order;

and a peer will finally be able to add

(*p*) his coronet of rank.

Let us deal with these heraldic adjuncts and essentials in that order.

THE SHIELD

Without the shield there can be neither coat of arms nor achievement. It is the shield upon the existence of which everything else hangs or depends, and it is the shield which is of first and greatest importance.

There are four or five historical coats of arms which consist of a plain shield of some single colour, but no presently existing British family has a right to such a coat of arms, and, that being the case, we are justified in saying that a shield or coat of arms must as a minimum consist of a coloured surface or background, this being termed the "field," and some figure or device or design thereupon, which forms the "charge" or "charges" if there be more than one. The outline of the rules relating both to the field and to the charges will be found detailed in a later chapter. Suffice it

here to say that the shield is the emblem
of the rank of gentility, it is the vehicle for
the display of the particular device which is
the token of the "technical" gentility of a
particular family (*i.e.* the male descendants of
a specified person or persons named in the
patent of the grant of arms creating the
nobility of which they are the emblem), and
the vehicle also for the display of the quarterings to denote inheritance of representation,
of marks of difference and distinction to
denote cadency, and for the display also of
arms of alliance by marriage, tenure, and
office. Briefly, to sum up, it is the shield
which is the important matter, and with which
the bulk of the rules of armory are concerned.

The shape of the shield adopted for pictorial representation is at the pleasure of the
wearer (*vide* Figs. 4, 5, 6, 7). One only needs
to give the warning to avoid anachronisms.

THE HELMET

Inasmuch as everybody during the period
of warfare in armour wore a helmet, so everybody who has a shield of arms has the right
to some helmet or other. There are certain
rules (which, however, only date from the
seventeenth century) regarding the form and
position of the helmet. These are (1) that
the royal helmet is of gold, is placed *affrontée*,
and is open, but with the opening guarded by

FIG. 4.

FIG. 5.

FIG. 6.

FIG. 7.

grilles or bars (*vide* Fig. 8) ; (2) that the helmet of a peer is of silver, is in profile, open, and

Fig. 8.

guarded by grilles of gold, with which metal it is garnished (*vide* Fig. 9) ; (3) that the helmet of a knight or baronet is of steel, is *affrontée*, with the visor open, and without grilles (*vide*

Figs. 10 and 11); (4) that the helmet of an esquire or gentleman is of steel, is in profile, and has the visor closed (*vide* Figs. 4, 5, 6 and 7). Both 3 and 4 may, if desired, be garnished with gold, this being the usual practice. Subject to these rules, the period, shape, style, and design of the helmet are at the pleasure of the wearer. Here as with the shield anachronism should be avoided. Do not draw a sixteenth-century helmet with a fourteenth-century shield when adopting the artistic style of the thirteenth century.

MANVS · HÆC   INIMICA·TYRANNIS

Fig. 9.

These rules for the helmet are unnecessary to the science, and I know of no argument in their favour. They produce striking absurdities, and some writers of authority and several of the best heraldic artists entirely ignore them. But for so long as they are officially recognised it seems to me they must be observed, though I devoutly hope their existence will be soon cut short.

THE MANTLING OR LAMBREQUIN

This is a cloth suspended from a point on the top of the helmet and hanging down the back of the wearer. Its purpose in real warfare was to save the armour from rust, to

FIG. 10.　　　　　　FIG. 11.

absorb the heat of the sun playing upon the metal armour, and, above all, to entangle the sword of an adversary and deaden the effect of a sword-cut. Originally a plain piece of cloth, any one who had been in the thick of the battle would soon find his

lambrequin cut and jagged, and no doubt
this would be esteemed. We find this idea
reflected in pictorial representations of arms,
for the plain cloth soon gives place to one cut
in fantastic forms. The heraldic artist quickly
seized upon the opportunity this afforded him,
and the pictorial lambrequin is now disposed
in exaggerated and flowing curves and folia-
tions on either side of the helmet and shield.
Heraldic rules lay down no set pattern, the
form and disposition of the mantling being
left to the fancy and invention of the artist
(*vide* almost any figure herein). There are
rules, however, with regard to colour. Originally throughout Europe the mantling was
of crimson cloth lined with white — and
was always so depicted. With few exceptions, this practice remained universal in
the United Kingdom until the close of the
seventeenth century, and in Scotland until
nearly the close of the nineteenth. But the
universal red and white mantling has given
place to a mantling of the "colours" of the
arms, the outside being of the colour, the
lining being of the metal. The use of livery
colours is now the rule throughout the United
Kingdom with these exceptions, viz., the
royal mantling is of gold lined with ermine;
the mantling of any peer whose arms are
Scottish is lined with ermine, and may be
either of his "colour" or of the crimson of his
Parliament robe.

THE WREATH OR TORSE

The crest must be attached to the helmet and lambrequin by some method of fastening of which the wreath or torse (*vide* many of the figures in this book) is the more usual. I believe it must have originated in the form of an ornament to hide the join of the crest on to the lambrequin. It was a skein of silk with a gold or silver cord twisted round it, and then placed as a fillet upon the helmet to cover the joining of the crest thereto.

Whilst old heraldic representations, *e.g.* the old Garter Stall Plates, and the designs of the best artists of the present day, still preserve the encircling form and appearance, the wreath in official representations, which have been naturally very widely dominant for a long period, has degenerated into a straight bar balanced on the top of the helmet (a perfectly impossible form for actual purposes) depicted in six alternate links of metal and colour, the former occurring first. This form may have some excuse when the wreath acts as a base for a crest used alone and without conjunction to a helmet, and no doubt it is from such usage that the present official form has been evolved, but it approaches the absurd when applied to a helmet. The wreath should be depicted alternately of the " colours " of the arms. The wreath is almost peculiar to British heraldry. Although a wreath appears with nine out of ten of the crests presently properly in use in the United Kingdom, its place is sometimes taken by a chapeau or a crest coronet.

The Chapeau

The chapeau (or cap of maintenance), occasionally also termed a cap of estate (Fig. 12),

Fig. 12.

is in reality, as its last-mentioned name indicates, nothing more than the cap of crimson velvet and fur which was anciently worn by all peers in Parliament as the sign of their right of peerage. This, for a peer, is now placed within the metal circlet and goes to make up his coronet; but the metal circlets are comparatively modern, none having been assigned to barons until the reign of Charles II., prior to which time the cap of estate was the only sign of their rank. Peers, therefore, very frequently placed a chapeau below their crests, and where this was done the wreath was omitted. Consequently a crest upon a chapeau became a very desirable possession. The use first extended to the members of the families of peers, who treated the chapeau as part of the crest to which they were entitled by inheritance, and the heraldic chapeau ceased to be exclusively a mark of the right of peerage. Then grants of crests upon chapeaus, either of the regulation colours, of crimson and ermine (Fig. 13) or of other tinctures, were made to men having no connection with the peerage, and during the seventeenth century a large number of such grants were made. The practice has, however, now ceased, and though upon sufficient proof of user a crest upon a chapeau might be matriculated in Lyon Register or confirmed by "Ulster," no grant is now made in that form except to peers, though, of course, a grant of such a crest to a peer would carry to all his descendants in the male line.

The Crest Coronet

The use of crest coronets is often supposed to have a similar origin to the crest chapeau, but, as a matter of fact, the crest coronet long antedates the coronet of rank. In fact, coronets encircling helmets antedate

Fig. 13.

crests themselves. They undoubtedly meant rank, and likely enough high rank, but not necessarily peerage rank, for they occur before peerages existed. Consequently their use with crests has been very widespread, and is very little short of universal in Continental heraldry. The oldest and most usual form is a plain gold circlet showing three strawberry leaves on the upper edge. This is termed a "ducal coronet" (Figs. 5 and 14). It should be distinguished from a Duke's coronet of rank, which shows five strawberry leaves. The granting of these ducal crest coronets has now entirely ceased, although occasionally one is met with in a matriculation or confirmation, but, of course, the right of descendants to use a crest coronet granted to an ancestor is never questioned. As genuine modern arms are gradually taking the place of bogus claims to ancient grants, the ducal crest coronets in use are decreasing in number, although at the zenith of the day of bogus heraldry these were as usual as the wreath, although the proportion of crest coronets to wreaths in ancient grants did not in any way justify such a disproportion.

The metal circlets of rank, or coronets, of peers of all degrees can be found in use as crest coronets, but the cases in which they so figure are very few indeed in number, and such usage is quite exceptional. There are, however, some other coronets of which heraldry has cognisance which are not coronets of rank. These are the mural (Fig. 15), the naval

(Fig. 16), the vallery (Fig. 18), the palisado, the antique (Fig. 17), and the celestial (Fig. 19). They are as frequently termed crowns as coronets, and if the term crown be used, then, perhaps, the term "civic" crown should be

Fig. 14.　　　　　　Fig. 15.

explained to make the list complete. This is merely a garland of oak leaves, and only appears as a charge. From its nature it could not be used as a crest coronet.

The *mural* crown is of some antiquity; it is a coronet made of masonry and may be granted of any tincture. It has always had a military significance, and though at one period it figures extensively in grants to people who apparently had no military connection, grants of crests issuing from a mural crown are sometimes made to military officers of the rank of general, although, of course, such a grant would devolve upon all descendants in the male line of the grantee.

The *naval* crown is less usual than the mural and more exclusively naval in connection. It is formed of a gold circlet, upon which are set alternately representations of the stern and of the sail of a ship. It is sometimes granted to admirals.

The crown *vallery* is a purely heraldic invention, the meaning of which is unknown, as are also its origin and the object of its existence. It is a modern conception, and is a circlet composed of a rim, and thereon set little pointed metal forms like an inverted shield in shape. This crest coronet can be obtained by anybody who worries the

Fig. 16.

College of Arms sufficiently. They dislike making such grants, but will generally succumb to importunity on this point.

The *palisado* crown is often treated as identical with the crown vallery, but it really is considered officially as distinct. It is formed

FIG. 17.   FIG. 18.

of palings attached to a metal circlet, these being much taller than the points of the crown vallery. This coronet also can be obtained by importunity, but it is modern in conception and ugly in appearance.

The *antique* crown, known also as the Saxon, the Scottish, and the Irish crown, and also as the Eastern crown, is a metal circlet surmounted by plain, tall, pointed spikes (Fig. 17). It is constantly used as a charge, but as a crest coronet in England it is now confined to grants of arms to those who have held high

office in India or the East. Under various of its other names little if any objection appears to be made to granting it in Scotland or Ireland.

The *celestial* crown is of the same form as the last one, except that a star is placed upon the point of each spike. It is not infrequently met

Fig. 19.

with as a charge, and as such figures in the arms recently granted to the Royal borough of Kensington (Fig. 19).

The Crest

Arms were in existence for a long period before we get any evidence of the use of a crest. This is the ornament which surmounts the helmet. The earliest forms are almost universally an animal, a demi-animal, or an animal's head. The use of a crest was very far indeed from general, or even usual, until the sixteenth century. In French heraldry the definite rule existed that only those families which were of tournament rank were entitled to crests. I know of no such rule in English heraldry, nor indeed do I see how "tournament rank" could be applied to English society, nor is it possible to exactly define what was in England the equivalent of that rank. But

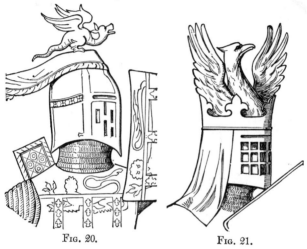

FIG. 20.　　　　　FIG. 21.

there can be no doubt whatever that some such idea must have operated, for until one gets beyond the period of tournaments and comes to the age of "paper" heraldry, one never finds a crest in use save by families of such sufficient station that one can rest assured they must have been of the required rank whatever were its qualifications. The lesser gentry all used arms, for which use there is ample evidence;

but whilst the possession of arms was universal amongst the land-owning class, the use of a crest was exceptional. I can find no contemporary evidence of the use of a crest in battle—the very nature and weight of a crest preclude the possibility—and there would seem to be little, if indeed any, room for doubt that crests belonged solely to the tournament and were never worn in actual warfare. It seems to me certain, however, that they were prized as a mark of high rank, which accounts for their importance for ceremonial purposes; but to me it seems equally certain that their use was confined to the tournament and to ceremonial.

When the paper stage of heraldry began, the use of heraldry was confined to ceremonial, and I confess to a strong suspicion that the heralds, seeking to induce the registration of arms after a period of laxity of control, held out the opportunity of the grant of the valued addition of a crest as an inducement to submission to official control. The inducement seems to have been very effective, for, as I have already said, there are now few coats of arms in existence to which no crest has been assigned. From the seventeenth century grants of arms (save as impalements or quarterings) have ceased to be made without the concurrent grant of a crest, and consequently the additional prestige attaching to the crest no longer has any weight. But it should, however, be noticed

that it is an absolute impossibility for a crest
to exist without a concurrent right to arms ;
and those people who assert a right to a crest,
whilst admitting no right to arms, are simply
assuming a position which is untenable and
wholly ridiculous. No person can ordinarily
have a right to more than one crest, unless a
right to a second or third has been expressly
granted, *e.g.* after the legal assumption of a
double name, or as an augmentation. Although
quarterings devolve through an heiress, a crest
does not.

The Motto

Mottoes had no place in the real armory of
actual warfare, and they are not met with
until late in the development of the science.

They originated upon the standard, occurring
doubtless as part of the badge which they may
have explained. But their appearance upon
the standard only occurs at the period when
these had become fictitious, by which I mean
a standard represented as an artistic drawing
and not as carried in battle or used in warfare.
It is not until late in the seventeenth century
that they become a usual part of a heraldic
achievement. At the present day even, they
form no part of a grant of arms in England.
Without any attempt at veto, the College of
Arms permits the selection of a motto at the
fancy of the grantee, and recognises no owner-
ship or prior claim in any particular motto or

form of words.   Unless a motto is selected by
the grantee the patent is issued without one,
but if one is selected, this, if the grantee desires,
will be painted and recorded with the arms
and crest granted, but it is not hereditary and
may be dropped or changed at pleasure.   Nor
is the possession of arms essential to the choice
or use of a motto in England.   The position
of the motto in a representation of an English
coat of arms is entirely a matter of personal
taste and choice.   It may be over the crest or
under the arms.

In Scotland the matter is entirely different.
The motto forms part of the grant and is
hereditary, and, moreover, the position in the
achievement which it is to occupy is specified
and must be adhered to.   This usually is over
the crest.

In Ireland the matter is halfway between
the practice in England and that in Scotland.
Whilst recognising and conforming to the
English absence of rule, the Irish procedure
considers a motto to be fixed and hereditary
where one has been made (as is now usual) a
part of the grant, or forms a part of an official
record.

SUPPORTERS

I am myself convinced that the origin of
supporters is to be traced to the badge, which
was in seals duplicated and depicted on either
side of the shield or crest in the vacant space

upon a seal left when the arms had been engraved. In the earliest seals—and these give us the first indication of supporters— these spaces are occupied by representations of badges, but primarily they do *not* " support " the shield or the helmet. At a later period

F<small>IG</small>. 22.

the artist makes them support the helmet for artistic reasons of disposition, and they then develop into the heraldic supporters of an achievement with which we are familiar.

From the period at which the artistic use of the badge has developed into the supporter, as we know it, the use of the supporter has been strictly confined. They are now granted (for life) to any Knight of the Garter, Thistle, or St. Patrick, and to any Knight Grand Cross (Fig. 22) or Knight Grand Commander of any Order who petitions for such a grant and pays the fees therefor, and they are also granted to

Fig. 23.

any peer (Figs. 23 and 26) to descend to such person as his specified peerage may devolve upon. In all three countries of the United Kingdom, warrants have been from time to time issued by the sovereign authorising the Kings of Arms to grant, by way of augmentation, supporters to specified individuals, either for life or with a hereditary limitation. These, however, are marks of royal favour, and are

Fig. 24.

quite exceptional. In Scotland, however, successive Lyon Kings of Arms have asserted and exercised the right to make grants of supporters at their discretion. This right, however, has been exercised very sparingly, and at the present time is practically used only in favour of the "heirs" of the many "minor barons," the chiefs of Scottish clans

FIG. 25.

or families (Figs. 24 and 25), and those to whom supporters would be granted in England. Ulster claims a similar right, but with one or two exceptions it has not been exercised outside the English limits.

Fig. 26.

The Compartment

Obviously supporters must stand upon something, and the English official practice has been uniformly to balance them upon a

golden scroll-work, which one heraldic writer
of repute happily terms a gas-bracket (Fig. 26).
In bygone times heraldic artists put the supporters to stand upon rocks, grassy mounds,
or (if suitable to their character) they were
made to issue from waves of the sea ; and the
whole thing could have been left as a matter
of artistic fancy and design were it not that in
England the royal "compartment" (the only
example) is specified to be adorned with the
rose, thistle, and shamrock (Fig. 8), and that
in Scotland there are some number of grants
or records of curious compartments, *e.g.* the
arms of Robertson, which are placed upon the
body of a wild man in chains, and the arms
of the Earl of Perth, which are on a compartment strewn with caltraps. But such cases
are so very few in number that one disregards
them save as to their being very honourable
exceptions ; and recognising that supporters
must stand on something, one has to adopt
the English "gas-bracket," or follow the older
artistic forms by substituting a resting-place
of a more appropriate character (Figs. 22, 23,
and 24).

The "Cri-de-Guerre"

"St. George for Merry England" was the
cry, shouting which the English soldiers went
into battle. "Crom a boo" was, undoubtedly,
the battle-cry of the FitzGeralds. This is now
used as their motto, and there are a number

of similar cases. The *cri-de-guerre* undoubtedly led to the insertion of mottoes on the old standards; but the genuine cases in which a *cri-de-guerre* existed, from which has since developed the heraldic usage thereof as an additional motto, are so few and so exceptional that they may be regarded simply as exceptions, and as far as the general student of armory is concerned, he need pay but little attention to the matter. For a family of modern origin to invent at a later date a form of words to palm off as a *cri-de-guerre* is too utterly contemptible to deserve attention.

THE STANDARD

Originally the standard represented the arms of a person as did his shield. But as the science of heraldry developed, and coats of arms became more intricate, it became general to adopt some simple object as a "badge," which would be readily recognised by the retainers. This badge was depicted upon the standard, and though the territorial lord would carry his proper arms upon his shield and surcoat, his standard, which the men he led would follow and muster by, had a representation of his badge or badges and not his arms. A very elaborate standard is shown in Fig. 27. The ground colour of the standard was of one or more tinctures, but was in every case of the colour of the livery which his followers actually

wore. At that period the colour of the
liveries was not necessarily, nor even usually,
in accordance with the arms, or what we now
know as the "livery colours" of the achievement.
At the end of the standard next to the staff
was always the cross of St. George on a
white ground—the badge of England. So
that friend and enemy alike knew that leader

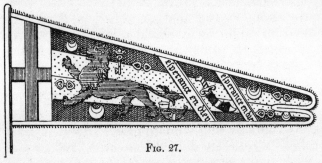

Fig. 27.

and men were English, although the other
figures on the standard might not be familiar.

To those who desire more detailed knowledge
of heraldic standards, I would make reference
to my book *Heraldic Badges* (published by
John Lane).

The Badge

Very little indeed is known about badges,
in spite of the fact that at one period (late
Plantagenet and early Tudor) the use of the
badge was of as great if not greater importance
than the use of arms. I have, as above

ndicated, treated the subject somewhat in detail in my book *Heraldic Badges*, to which I would refer those who desire more extended knowledge. Suffice it here to say that as arms became intricate and numerous, and as they of necessity in consequence became less easy for the illiterate to differentiate, the very necessities of camp life and actual warfare demanded and resulted in the "standards" being made of the colours of the liveries the re-

Fig. 28.

ainers wore, and in such standards showing the simple device or "badge" which the leader adopted for the purpose of ready recognition by his retainers (Figs. 28 and 29). This badge was embroidered back and breast or on the sleeve of the jackets worn by his retainers, and badges of well-known men were household words.

When the English army ceased to be collected on feudal lines by the tenants in capite of the king, but was recruited directly in the name of the king, badges ceased to be a necessity and their use de-

Fig. 29.

lined. Those who had badges recorded them as crests, and the ancient families who owned badges have gradually become almost extinct.

In these days of absurd pedigree pretension
and bogus pedigree claims (the bogus claimant
always talks the loudest), there are not many
who fully recognise the fact that nowadays a
male pedigree back to the Conquest is a wild
exception, and that male descent even as far
back as Tudor times is most exceptional, even
amongst those landed and titled families who
are now generally regarded as of ancient date.
In the whole of the United Kingdom, there are
probably not more than two hundred families
now of landed and county rank who trace
male descent from ancestors of that rank in
Plantagenet days.   When one has ranged
twenty English families who can carry such a
descent back to the Conquest, the list has been
about exhausted.

The inevitable result has been that no
standards having been recorded after that
period, no new badges were called into being,
and so the use of the badge has been attenuated
to a point little short of extinction.   The
purpose of a badge is that it shall be worn by
retainers and marked upon one's possessions,
and the modern fashion has been to substitute
the crest for the real purposes of the badge.
A truer appreciation of their several uses has
induced the College of Arms to resume the
granting of badges, and the grant of a badge
involves the creation and record of a standard.
the grant being so worded that it becomes permissible to depict and use the badge either upon

the standard or else alone as a badge. The grant of a badge being therefore now a matter possible to obtain, there remains no excuse for the improper use of the crest upon the livery or livery buttons of a servant.

AUGMENTATIONS

These, as the name would imply, are *additions* to an existing heraldic achievement (previously obtained by "purchase!") granted by favour of the sovereign to commemorate some notable service. The bulk of the tales one hears of arms granted as a reward for this, that, or the other service are simply unadulterated rubbish. The *real* augmentations are all perfectly well known, and the warrants from various sovereigns therefor properly recorded. Instances

FIG. 30.

may be found in any peerage book, in the arms of the Duke of Wellington, Earl Nelson, Viscount Gough, or (to quote the most recent examples), Viscount Kitchener, who, like Lord

Gough, has had two separate warrants, and **Sir Frederick Treves, Bt.** Why no augmentation has ever been conferred upon Earl Roberts, K.G., remains an absolute mystery.

An augmentation may take the form of some addition to the shield (Figs. 30 and 31), or of an additional crest or of supporters, and though the recipient must already possess, or acquire at his own expense, arms and crest, the actual grant of the augmentation is made without payment of any fee.

There are one or two instances, *e.g.* the arms of Carlos granted by King Charles II. to his companion in the oak tree at Boscobel, where the reward has taken the form of the gift of arms. Such a case, though equally honourable, is not really an "augmentation," and such cases are quite exceptional, and probably, all told, are not a dozen in number. The inescutcheon of Ulster borne by baronets of England, Ireland, Great

Fig. 31.

Britain, and the United Kingdom (Fig. 23), is an augmentation.

THE CIRCLETS OF KNIGHTHOOD

A knight, commander, or companion, of any Order may place around his shield the circlet bearing the motto of the Order which appears upon the star he is entitled to wear. This for Knights of the Garter is a representation of the Garter (Fig. 8), but in the case of other Orders is a plain circlet (Figs. 9, 11, 22) of differing but specified colours, carrying in gold letters the motto of his Order. Knights of the *military* (but *not* the civil) division of the Order of the Bath use also a wreath of laurel (Fig. 16). Only one circlet, that of the highest Order, is used at a time.

COLLARS OF KNIGHTHOOD

Knights of the Garter, Thistle, and St. Patrick, and all other Knights Grand Cross or Knights Grand Commanders, who as such are entitled to wear a " collar " of their Order, have a right to place it around their arms (Figs. 8, 9, 22). It should be disposed *outside* the circlet, and in a full representation *all* collars to which the right exists are displayed, the inner ones being the highest in rank.

Coronets of Rank

Coronets have now been assigned to all degrees of the peerage. They all consist of

Fig. 32.

Fig. 33.

gilt metal circlets of varying patterns (Duke, Fig. 32; Marquess, Fig. 33; Earl, Fig. 34; Viscount, Fig. 35; Baron, Fig. 36) enclosing a red velvet cap lined with fur, the cap being,

Fig. 34.

Fig. 35.

as already stated, the real sign of right of peerage, the metal circlet merely denoting the particular rank in the peerage.

To denote and commemorate the fact that he is also a peer, a cap of maintenance is always carried (by a peer, generally a great officer of State or Cabinet minister) before the

sovereign when he proceeds to Parliament, but the English crown differs from a peer's coronet by being enclosed by the crossed arches (Fig. 37). The Prince of Wales has a single arch (Fig. 38). The other royal coronets differ only from

FIG. 36.

the coronet of a peer in the design of the circlet (Fig. 39).

FIG. 37.

Fig. 38.

FIG. 39.

CHAPTER V

HOW TO USE A COAT OF ARMS

To any person desiring to use arms, and who has satisfied himself of his right to a coat of arms, I would offer certain remarks. There are certain points to be borne in mind:

1. The arms should be displayed correctly, so that there shall be no opportunity for criticism.
2. The device selected should be suitable to the opportunity, and of the character usually adopted by others for the purpose.
3. Subject to the foregoing qualification, then it should be remembered that the use of heraldic devices is constant and usual, it might be termed wholesale, at every opportunity by that class of society with whom the possession of arms is a matter of course and not a matter of ostentation; and, providing the use of heraldic insignia is not anachronistic in its character, it is difficult if not impossible to make too great a use of genuine heraldic emblems. One instance will show what I mean by anachronistic.

The display of heraldic devices—carved or in stained glass—is common as a matter of internal decoration, but such devices would look egregiously absurd if placed in a room designed and decorated in the "Adam" style.

External Architectural Use.—Arms may be properly displayed on an architectural gateway, above a doorway, on a gable, or upon metal entrance-gates. In such a case a simple shield of the arms for the name is most appropriate, though if architectural or artistic reasons exist, a more elaborate and complete achievement might be used. A crest and motto alone would look silly.

If an addition is made to a house, it is a matter of interest to future successors to date that addition by placing in some suitable position a shield of the arms of husband and wife, conjoined to show in which lifetime the addition was made.

Internal Decoration.—Up to the beginning of the eighteenth century, armorial devices were placed at every opportunity in the decoration of a house, and such decoration generally remains in houses dating from an earlier period. The chief opportunities made use of appear to be the fireplaces, the ceilings, the windows, and the panels.

Fireplaces.—If the attempt is made to reproduce a past period with an open fireplace and a dog-grate, the fireplace should be surmounted by a modelled representation of the full heraldic achievement. This was, unless carved in oak, usually represented in its proper heraldic colours. The arms or a badge are often seen on the iron back of the dog-grate.

Ceilings.—The bulk of Tudor and Jacobean ceilings are of plaster, divided by some design of moulding into compartments. The spaces available were usually occupied by a repetition of a badge or an alternation of several badges. The simple figure of the badge, which has often been taken to be pure ornament, its heraldic nature being overlooked, has led to the designing of Tudor and Jacobean ceilings on the ground of pure ornament alone. Undoubted ceilings of that period were usually heraldic.

Windows.—The heraldic stained glass for a window, perhaps more than anything else, needs to be designed by an architect, so that it shall conform to the style and character of the other decoration.

Panels.—In old houses one constantly meets in the hall, or the gallery, or the dining-room, with a series of heraldic panels, carved in oak, modelled in plaster, or set up in stone. It is seldom that such a series is mere duplication of a single coat. As a rule, it will be found either that the series is (*a*) a set of shields showing the conjoined arms of husband and wife, one for each generation through which the house has devolved, or (*b*) a set of shields showing the quarterings, one by one, to which the family lay claim. I have never come across a series which did not explain itself in some such manner, or which proved on examination to be mere haphazard decoration.

Other forms such a series might suitably take would be a series of "matches," that is a conjoined shield for every marriage through which descent is traced, or a series of shields of the arms of different families from whom descent can be shown, regardless of whether these were or were not inherited as quarterings. But in ancient houses where a series exists, it will be found they are of the shield only (or shield and coronet). I have never seen a series in which helmets and crests had been introduced; but it will always be found that over the fireplace there is a huge representation of the full achievement, arms, crest, supporters, helmet, and mantling with quarterings and impalement, whatever may exist.

Carriages.—Except upon state coaches, which are reserved for court and official purposes, the day is past (unfortunately for heraldry) when vehicles were made the opportunity for the display of the full achievement in a conspicuous size. At the present day a small shield, helmet, mantling, crest, and motto, or else a shield, crest, and motto, or more frequently crest and motto only, is all that is used even on a brougham or car.

Plate.—The crest only is all that one finds

engraved upon spoons and forks, but on larger pieces of plate, *e.g.* on a salver, the opportunity is usually taken of engraving the whole achievement. Whilst forks and spoons are con-

FIG. 40.

stantly renewed, and of necessity treated with scant ceremony, a salver usually lasts for many generations. Consequently, it adds to the interest of a collection of plate if the conjoined arms of husband and wife are engraved upon it, This tells its history in the family, for whilst many people, many different families even, may use the same crest or even the same arms and crest, it is rare indeed that an impaled coat would be correct for more than a single match.

Livery Buttons.—These should show the badge and not the crest.

Book-Plates.—The smallest library, if the books are of any character more permanent than a novel, deserves a book-plate. Many borrowed books have been returned in consequence of the appearance of the owner's book-plate therein, which otherwise would have remained amongst the borrower's own collections. A book-plate should be a work of art, and an ordinary shop production looks paltry when compared with a design by a good artist (Fig. 40). In the past as in the present the full achievement is found on the best plates, and a book label showing only a crest merely looks cheap, whilst its possessor may really have been trying to avoid ostentation.

Seals.—Few people trouble to make a careful impression of a seal in wax when actually using it. It is not easy, moreover, to rival the beautiful impression which the seal-cutter always supplies with the seal. Consequently, a seal should never be crowded with detail. Unnecessary quarterings are a mistake, and probably most satisfaction will result from the crest only on a signet ring, and the shield only upon a fob or desk seal, unless this be of large size; and there are but few legitimate opportunities of using a large seal except upon deeds.

CHAPTER VI

THE CONJUNCTION OF THE ARMS
OF MAN AND WIFE

THERE are several ways in which this is done, and if arms exist for the family from which

the wife is descended, there can be no question
that the arms of husband and wife should be
borne in a conjoined form during their joint
lives.   Wherever the conjoined arms are
permanently placed as a record or memorial
of the match, of course they properly remain,
but, on a seal for example, or on a carriage
where the point is *use* and, so to speak,
advertisement of rank and not *record*, there
the conjoined arms should give place to the
simple arms of the man, or the correct arms
of a widow, as the case may be.

To know how arms should be conjoined it
is first necessary to determine whether or not
the wife is an "heiress in blood" according
to the heraldic definition.

No woman can be an heiress in the lifetime
of her father, save in one exceptional case,
which occurs so rarely that it need not be
considered.

After the death of her father, a woman is
an heiress if she be an only child, or a
coheiress if she has sisters but has never had
a brother.   If all brothers have died without
leaving any issue at all, the woman is an
heiress or coheiress, but if a brother has left a
daughter, then that daughter is an heiress and
not her aunt.

'When the wife is not an heiress, the arms of
husband and wife are conjoined by *impalement*
(Fig. 41).

To impale two coats the shield is divided

by a perpendicular line down the centre. The entire arms of the husband are placed on the *dexter* side, and the pronominal arms of the wife are placed on the *sinister* side. The only exception is that if either coat is surrounded by a bordure this is omitted down the centre of the shield.

As one looks at a shield the dexter side is

FIG. 41.   FIG. 42.

the left-hand side and the sinister is the right-hand side, because, of course, it should be remembered that a shield is supposed to be carried in front of one, which naturally reverses the position.

When the wife is an heiress impalement is not made use of, but the husband places the wife's arms on a small escutcheon super-imposed on the centre of his own (Fig. 42).

This is termed an escutcheon of pretence, because it signifies that the husband "pretends" to the representation of his wife's family.

It is not usual to display the quarterings of a wife's family in an impalement, but it is correct to do so on an escutcheon of pretence. But if the wife's family, because of a compound name or for any other reason, have a compound subquarterly coat, such a coat cannot be divided and must all be impaled. Similarly, a Scottish coat matriculated with quarterings within a bordure is not regarded as divisible.

Fig. 43.

If the husband be a bishop or have other arms of office, or if as a knight of an order he is entitled to encircle his arms with any circlet of knighthood, he uses two shields inclined towards each other (Fig. 43). On the dexter is his official coat impaled with his personal arms (or, as the case may be, his own arms within his circlet of knighthood), and on the sinister shield his personal arms are repeated, impaled with those of the wife or (if she be an heiress) with hers in pretence. The arms of a peer and his wife (here not an heiress) are conjoined, as in Fig. 44; of a commoner married to a peeress in her own right, as in Fig. 45; and of a peer married to a peeress in her own right, as in Fig. 46.

Fig. 44.

Although the arms of several wives may be set up in the way the rules of heraldry provide as a matter of record or memorial, it is quite incorrect to *use* the arms of two wives at the same time.

Fig. 45.

FIG. 46.

CHAPTER VII

THE ARMS OF A LADY

THE rules of heraldry forbid to any lady, save a Queen regnant, the use of shield, crest, motto, helmet, or mantling in her own right. She is, however, permitted before marriage to display the arms of her family upon a lozenge (Fig. 47).

During marriage the real position heraldically is that the identity of the wife is merged in that of the husband, who bears impaled or in pretence the arms of his wife's family for her (Figs. 41 and 42). If it be necessary, *e.g.* on a

FIG. 47.

hatchment, to depict the arms of a married woman to signify her separate person, this is done by placing the arms of the husband and wife on a shield as they would ordinarily be borne. This shield is then represented as suspended by and from a ribbon, the helmet, crest, and motto being omitted.

Fig. 48.

A widow reverts to the lozenge, placing thereupon the arms of her deceased husband conjoined with those of her own family as her husband bore them, either impaled (Fig. 48) or with hers in pretence (Fig. 49), as circumstances dictate.

A woman may use a badge, and a peeress,

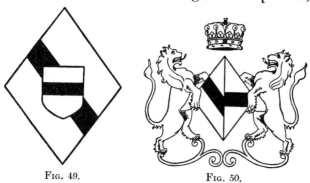

Fig. 49.   Fig. 50.

whilst such, uses supporters (Fig. 50, which shows the arms of a widowed peeress). There

are a few Scottish cases in which ladies, not
being peeresses, have inherited supporters, but
they are very uncommon.

CHAPTER VIII

QUARTERINGS

THE importance and value of heraldic quarterings is vastly over-rated by those lacking
intimate experience of armory. The possession of them is due to accident, and means
practically nothing. When quartering came
into vogue, which it did at an early period of
heraldry, a man marrying a great heiress begot
a son, who probably inherited more from his
mother than from his father, and so naturally
wished to bear the arms of both families, so
he quartered them. So long as quarterings
indicated such inheritances and such conjoined
representation of different families' quarterings, the desire to quarter was intelligible, but
the legal position naturally followed that, if
quartering meant representation by virtue of
descent from heiresses, as it naturally did, then,
as a corollary, a man might quarter the arms
of every heiress, great or small, from whom
he descended, and as, legally, "representation"
makes the heiress and not her possessions,

the right to quarterings simply means the technical representation of so many heiresses.

A well-known family, recently extinct in the male line, had a proved male descent back to the Norman period. Generation after generation they married women of good birth and high rank, but, as none of the wives happened to be heiresses, that family, I believe, never inherited a single quartering, though they were as well born and as well bred as any family in the kingdom.

On the other hand, a man of no pedigree obtained a grant of arms and married an only child of a younger son of a cadet branch of an ancient family. His children have inherited some sixty to seventy quarterings through their mother, although their technical "nobility" is less than thirty years old.

But so long as their value is not over-estimated, quarterings are a matter of considerable interest. Let us take the simplest case. A man entitled to arms marries an heiress who also is entitled to arms, and bears her arms on an escutcheon of pretence, as explained in the previous chapters (Fig. 42). The children of the marriage after the death of the mother are entitled to quarter the two coats of arms. This they do by dividing the shield into four equal parts by intersecting lines, one perpendicular, and one horizontal. The dexter top quarter is No. 1 ; the sinister top quarter is No. 2 ; the dexter bottom corner is No. 3; the sinister bottom corner is No. 4. The arms of the father are then placed in No.

1 and repeated in No. 4, whilst the arms of the mother are placed in Nos. 2 and 3 (Fig. 51).

Now, let us assume that a son of that marriage marries another heiress. In the centre of his own quarterly coat he will bear her arms on an escutcheon of pretence (Fig. 52). His children, being entitled to quarter their mother's arms, will place them in the third quartering, omitting (to make room for them) the repetition of their grandmother's arms (Fig. 53).

Fig. 51.

The arms of a later heiress would go into the fourth quarter.

But you may have any number of quarters on a shield, and they are counted from dexter to sinister, beginning with the first row along the top of the shield, then the next row, and so on.

Fig. 52.

The number of quarterings in a row, and the number of rows to be used to display a given number of quarterings, is a matter of choice, depending upon convenience dictated by the number and the shape of the shield.

If an heiress represent a family with quarterings, her children are entitled to add to their paternal quarterings the whole of those of their mother's family.

To determine the order of the quarterings one resorts to the pedigree. First comes the most modern grant of arms for the surname then in use, then the next most modern one. One has to explain this in these days of frequent changes of name and consequent exemplifications of various arms. Say these run—1. Brown-Smith under a royal license in 1880; 2. Brown-Jones under a royal license in 1800; whilst the

FIG. 53.

real male descent is Robinson, the arms for which would be No. 3.

The next step is to follow the male descent back to the earliest match with an heiress. Let us suppose she was a Miss Wilson— possessing also a quartering for Price. This would mean that the fourth quartering would be Wilson, the fifth Price. Suppose the next heiress was a Miss Perkins, having ten other quarterings. Perkins would then be No. 6, and the ten other quarterings would follow as Nos. 7 to 16.

It is always permissible to repeat the first quartering as the last and final one, if this helps to make up an even number or a conveniently divisible number, but only the first may be repeated.

Grand quarterings, *i.e.* an ordinary quartering

Fig. 54.

itself subdivided into quarterings, only occur (Fig. 54) in English heraldry when a compound and indivisible coat occurs, *e.g.* a compound coat exemplified under a royal license for a double name.

Upon proof made and registered of descent from an heiress and of the consequent representation, the right to quarter the arms of that heiress is at once officially admitted and certified, and if the heiress were not entitled to arms, a grant of a quartering can be obtained to bear in significance of the representation of her family.

The rules cited above apply to English and Irish arms, they do not apply to Scottish armory. In Lyon Office the right to quarter as accruing *ipso facto* from the mere representation of an heiress is not recognised without a rematriculation of the arms with the quartering introduced. Whilst the theory of

Fig. 55.

representation as applied to quarterings is recognised in actual practice, quartering is discouraged in Scotland unless substantial reason in the form of land or wealth justifies the addition. Moreover, in Scotland a quartered shield has only four quarters, and those quarters must be subquartered if other arms are to be introduced. This form of marshalling is termed "counter-quartering" or quartering by "grand-quarters" (Fig. 55). In the end it becomes far more complicated and confusing than the English method. There are no hard and fast rules in Scotland to control the disposition of the quarterings, the "rematriculation" validating whatever arrangement may seem most suitable under the circumstances of the particular case.

A Scottish coat after matriculation being indivisible until superseded by rematriculation must be treated as one quartering if it occurs in an English scheme. The result is sometimes curious; but Scottish law conflicts with English in many matters besides heraldry.

CHAPTER IX

MARKS OF DIFFERENCE AND DISTINCTION

THE heraldic marks which are made use of to differentiate amongst those who are entitled to the same arms are divided into marks of "difference" and marks of "distinction."

MARKS OF DIFFERENCE OR CADENCY

These are used to advertise the seniority in the family of its different members by legitimate male descent. Not only are the marks different in England and Scotland, but the whole system of their application is different.

In England their use is not compulsory,

but they are assumed or discarded at the
pleasure of the wearer without official act of

FIG. 56.

authorisation, they are changed as the circumstances of the descent and seniority change
(*e.g.* by the extinction of a senior line), and
their use is a matter of caprice, save that if
they are used they
should and are re-
quired to be used
correctly.

The unmarked coat
belongs to the heir
male of the grantee.
The eldest son *in the
lifetime of his father*
places across the top
of his shield a label or
file of three points
(Fig. 56 *a*). His eldest
son uses a label of five
points *in the lifetime
of his grandfather*.

The sign of the se-
cond son is a crescent

FIG. 57.

(Fig. 56 *b*), of the third a mullet (Fig. 56 *c*), of
the fourth a martlet (Fig. 56 *d*), of the fifth an
annulet (Fig. 56 *e*), of the sixth a fleur-de-lis
(Fig. 56 *f*).

The second son of a second son, for example, would use a crescent charged upon a crescent (Fig. 57), and so on.

These difference marks are placed upon the shield in any convenient position, usually in the centre near the top ("in the centre chief"), and they are quite small in size and must

Fig. 58.　　　　　　　Fig. 59.

never be large enough to be mistaken for a charge (*i.e.* a component part) of the shield.

They may be of any colour, the attempt usually being to select a tincture which does not occur in the arms.

The introduction of a quartering wipes out all difference marks which accrued prior to its introduction, as the quartering is in itself sufficient difference, and a fresh start is made from that point. Upon a quarterly coat the difference mark is placed on a dividing line to show that it relates to the whole shield and not to a single quartering (Fig. 57). A quartering may, however, be inherited, subject to a difference mark, but this would usually be discarded unless some special reason existed for its continuance.

The Scottish system is based upon the necessity imposed upon cadets to rematriculate. With few exceptions, the first cadet version matriculated has assigned a plain bordure to the coat. In all subsequent cadet matriculations of those arms the change is made by a variation of that bordure. As the

Fig. 60.

Scottish system is not a matter at the pleasure of the wearer but involves official matriculation, and as the system which governs the variation of the bordures is highly technical and subject to modification according to circumstances, it is not possible in the limited scope of the present work to discuss it in detail. But Figs. 59, 60, and 61 are different versions of the original Scottish coat, Fig. 58, and are typical of the system.

The Irish system is identical with the English rules.

FIG. 61.

MARKS OF DISTINCTION

These are used to signify (*a*) absence of blood descent (*b*) illegitimacy.

Marks for the former purpose are unknown in Scotland and Ireland. They are used in England, when under a will or settlement requiring the assumption of name and arms a royal license is issued to a person who can show no descent in the male or female line from the family whose arms are then exemplified. Some mark is then added to the arms and to the crest to advertise this fact. There are no rules as to what these marks shall be, and they of course depend upon the terms of the patent of exemplification. They are, however, most frequently a canton and a cross crosslet respectively. With regard to the signs of bastardy, there is not, and never has been, and it is impossible there ever can be, such a thing as a " bar sinister."

The colloquialism is a corruption of the French term *barre-sinistre*. An English " bar " is a totally different thing from the French *barre*, which is the equivalent of the English " bend."

A bend sinister used to be the English sign of illegitimacy, and consequently a bend sinister never occurs with any other meaning. But it has long been entirely discarded, and I know of no ancient coat which has survived to the present day in which it occurs with that meaning.

There is no rule or law of heraldry which prescribes what shall be the mark to denote illegitimacy; different figures have been used at different periods and under varying circumstances. The present practice in England —stereotyped now by an invariable usage of over a century—is to place a bordure wavy round the shield and to debruise the crest usually but not always by a *bendlet sinister wavy*.

The bordure wavy does not mean illegitimacy in Scotland, where it merely denotes cadency. In Scotland the present practice is to place a *bordure compony* round the arms, *i.e.* a bordure composed of *one row* of alternating pieces of a colour and a metal. The bordure compony (or gobony) has also been used in England as a sign of bastardy, and also on the Continent, but it has also been used without that meaning. In Scotland the crest is not marked in any way.

In Ireland a bordure compony is sometimes used, but more usually a bordure wavy. A change of some kind is made in the crest, but this change follows no fixed rules.

In no case does a bastard inherit even a bastardised version of the arms of either father or mother. He requires a royal license to bear the name and arms, which can only be obtained on very stringent proof of paternity, and which is only granted as to the arms with such "due and proper marks of distinction" as may be exemplified and recorded by the Officers of Arms. It is always open to a bastard not to disclose his illegitimacy or claim any descent, but to petition for a grant of arms *de novo* to be made to him. The fees on a grant are less than upon a royal license and exemplification, and a new grant of a technically different coat (which may be very similar to the old one) will contain no marks of bastardy. This opportunity is open to all of illegitimate birth, save those who, under a will or settlement, are required to assume the name and arms of a specified family from whom they are not legitimately descended.

CHAPTER X

THE DETAILS OF THE SHIELD—THE FIELD

HITHERTO, I have endeavoured as far as was possible to avoid the intricate technicalities of the science of heraldry, my effort being to supply such details in general outline as are likely to be needed by an inquirer who desires to know how to use his own coat of arms, and how to apply it to different purposes without being involved in a profound study of heraldry, for which few have time and still fewer the inclination. I am convinced that the absence of practical information in handbooks hitherto available, which deal too exclusively with the mere antiquarian side of armory, is the cause of the bulk of heraldic mistakes, and also the cause of the decline of interest in heraldry, which was so marked prior to the recent revival. A decline of interest does not mean a decline in the extent of usage, rather otherwise, for whilst any prestige in the possession of arms continues, a decline of interest and of practical knowledge simply results in an increase of spurious heraldry. The result of that is a decline in its prestige.

But even in a work of the limited scope of this little volume, it seems desirable to touch briefly upon the more important points of the technical science, although for any adequate knowledge of the science—my three or four remaining chapters can form but a mere introduction to a more detailed work on the subject—either my own *Art of Heraldry* or the volumes of some other writer upon the subject should be consulted. There are some number now in the market.

A coat of arms, *i.e.* the device upon a shield, consists of two parts, "the field" and

the charge or charges. I do not here refer to a shield, which by reason of impalement or quarterings displays many coats marshalled together.

The "field" is the tincture of the background of the shield upon which the charge or device is displayed. There

FIG. 62.

are one or two historical coats which consist of a field of a single colour without a charge (Fig. 62). But these are so exceptional that they can be disregarded.

The tinctures which are available are divided into colours, metals, and furs.

COLOURS

These are gules, azure, sable, vert, and purpure—the heraldic names for red, blue, black, green, and purple respectively.

METALS

These are "or" and "argent"—the heraldic names respectively for gold and silver. "Or" is usually depicted in actual gold, though not infrequently yellow is used in its place. "Argent" is most frequently depicted white, though occasionally the metal (in actual practice aluminium) takes the place of white.

FIGS. 63, 64.   FIG. 65.   FIG. 66.

FURS

The principal furs are "ermine" (a white ground with black ermine spots) (Figs. 62 and 63), ermines (a black ground with white spots) (Fig. 64), erminois (a gold ground with black spots), vair (alternate shield-shaped divisions of blue and white) (Fig. 65), and potent (as the last, but the divisions taking the shape of the head of a crutch) (Fig. 66).

Originally ermine and vair were the only furs in use. Potent is a corrupted derivative of vair, and ermines and erminois are variations of ermine of modern manufacture but of not infrequent use. There is still another variety, "pean," which is a black ground with gold spots.

In addition, there are little intricacies of difference, which are supposed to create "erminites," "miniver," "grosvair," "counter-vair," "counter-potent," and such like varieties and terms, but they are met with but once or twice in a lifetime, and are largely the imaginations of heraldic writers.

Continental heraldry has other additions to make to the lists, alike of colours, metals, and furs, but if one begins to include the terms of foreign heraldry, one needs pursue it a long and tedious way.

When arms are represented in colour, as is their intention, that difficulty does not exist which at once emerges when arms are depicted in black or white, or represented in a medium in which colour is impossible. Anciently in such cases no attempt was made to indicate the colours save in matters of record, when a contraction, *e.g.* "sa," "arg," "vt," would be written upon the drawing. Such a drawing is termed a "trick," and for all official purposes arms now, as they always have been, are so "tricked" or else represented in colour. Official heraldry knows nothing of "tincture lines" (*vide* Fig. 8), which are an engraver's invention of the seventeenth century. Within the last decade their use seems almost by the common consent of heraldic artists of repute to have ceased, but in the intervening period their usage was so absolutely universal that it is necessary to subjoin the diagram below to show the tinctured lines which were accepted (Fig. 67).

The field may be of a single metal, a single colour, or a single fur, and it may here be remarked that no heraldic meaning or significance attaches to any of them, and all rank on a level.

A field may be of two or more tinctures, but it seldom occurs of more than two, though the division of the shield may mean an alternation of many pieces.

The two tinctures may be two colours, two

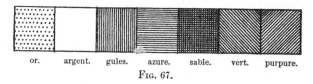

| or. | argent. | gules. | azure. | sable. | vert. | purpure. |

FIG. 67.

metals, or two furs (for neither is imposed upon the other), or it may be of metal and colour, metal and fur, or colour and fur.

Whilst coats without a charge are rare indeed where the field is a single tincture, such coats are quite ordinary where the field is of two tinctures, *e.g.* the arms of Campbell, which are "gyronny, or and sable," or those of Waldegrave, which are "per pale, argent and gules."

The two tinctures may be disposed per pale, per fesse, per bend, per chevron, per cross (quarterly), or gyronny, in other words, divided into two parts by a partition line drawn in the direction occupied by the pale, the fesse, the bend, the chevron, the cross, or the gyron, figures which will be described amongst the "charges" dealt with in the next chapter.

The field may be "paly (Fig. 68)," "barry," "bendy," "chevrony" (Fig. 69), etc., *i.e.* divided into a number of divisions (usually six, unless otherwise specified) made by a succession of partition lines disposed in the directions indicated.

Fig. 68.

Fig. 69.

These divisions may be more numerous, approximating in dimension to the diminutives of the figures referred to when the field is termed, *e.g.* barruly.

The partition lines in a field are most frequently plain, but all heraldic partition lines are subject to certain variations, which the subjoined diagram enumerates and explains (Fig. 70).

A field divided per bend sinister (a frequent

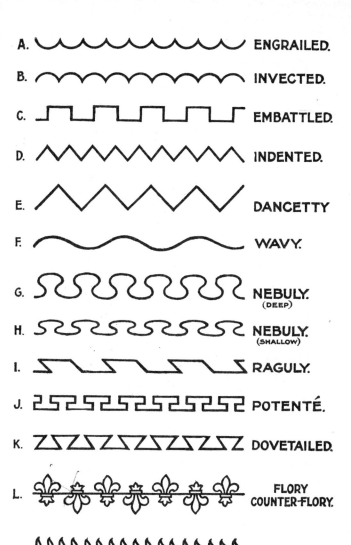

A. ENGRAILED.

B. INVECTED.

C. EMBATTLED.

D. INDENTED.

E. DANCETTY

F. WAVY.

G. NEBULY.
(DEEP)

H. NEBULY.
(SHALLOW)

I. RAGULY.

J. POTENTÉ.

K. DOVETAILED.

L. FLORY
COUNTER-FLORY.

M. RAYONNÉ.

FIG. 70.

occurrence particularly in Welsh arms) carries
no suggestion of illegitimacy.

A field covered with a succession of small
charges is said to be semé of them, but there
are certain special terms in use, thus semé-
de-lis means a succession of fleurs-de-lis
(Fig. 71); "crusuly" is equivalent to semé of
cross crosslets (Fig. 72); "gutté" means

Fig. 71.   Fig. 72.

covered with drops, the terms in use being
gutté-d'eau when white, gutté-de-poix (black),
gutté-d'or (gold), gutté-de-larmes (blue), gutté-
de-sang (red), gutté-d'huile (green).

CHAPTER XI

HERALDIC CHARGES—THE ORDINARIES, ETC.

THE charge is the figure or figures disposed
upon the field which together with that make
up the coat of arms.

ORNAT PRUDENTIA FORTEM

Fig. 73.

VI·ET·VIRTUTE

Fig. 74.

Devant si je puis

En espoir je vive attendant grace

Fig. 75.

UNG·ROY·UNG·FOY·UNG·LOY

Fig. 76.

Of these the most important are the set of figures which are usually referred to as the "ordinaries." There are various classifications of these figures, which are generally divided into ordinaries and subordinaries. But the classifications of different writers seldom agree, and I myself quite fail to see any real necessity for the existence of any classification at all. Heraldic writers, I consider, have always been much too prone to make these classifications, and to invent and apply thereto rules which are never recognised and conformed to in official heraldry.

The principal ordinaries about which there can be no dispute are :—

> The pale (Fig. 73).
> The fesse (Fig. 74).
> The bend (Fig. 75).
> The cross (Fig. 76).
> The saltire (Fig. 58).
> The chevron (Fig. 77).
> The pile (Fig. 78).
> The chief (Fig. 79).
> The quarter (Fig. 80).

The first three are simple bands which cross the shield—being a third thereof or rather less in width—respectively, perpendicularly, horizontally, and diagonally. The bend may be either dexter or sinister, but the latter is hardly ever met with.

The cross is familiar to every one.

FIG. 77.

FIG. 78.

FIG. 79.

FIG. 80.

The saltire is merely the cross set diagonally
—St. Andrew's Cross.

The chevron is another well-known figure,
and the pile can be most readily explained by
a reference to Fig. 78.

FIG. 81.   FIG. 82.

The chief is a band occupying the top part
of the shield (Figs. 5 and 79).

The quarter needs no explanation.

Most of these figures have diminutives, but
the "diminutive" (unless it be the canton) is
seldom met with singly, and is usually found
double or treble.

The diminutive of the pale is the pallet, of

the bend the bendlet (Fig. 84), of the saltire the gyron, and of the chevron the chevronel (Figs. 4 and 82), whilst the canton is the diminutive of the quarter, its own diminutive being the chequer.

The pile and the chief have no diminutives.

Fig. 83.

Fig. 84.

The fesse if duplicated in a coat becomes a bar (Fig. 73), though there is little difference in the size of a fesse and a bar. The diminutive of the bar is the barrulet, and of the barrulet the "bar-gemel," which, as its name implies, is really a barrulet divided into two.

There are other purely heraldic figures sometimes classed with the ordinaries, of which

FIG. 85.

FIG. 86.

FIG. 87.

FIG. 88.

the more important are the lozenge (Figs. 6 and 101), the mascle (Fig. 83), the fret (Fig. 84), the flaunch (Fig. 85), the inescutcheon, the orle (Fig. 86), the tressure (Fig. 87), the bordure, the pall or shakefork (Fig. 88).

The cross, the pale, the bend (Fig. 81), the fesse, the bar, the saltire, the chevron (Fig. 89), may all be found cottised, singly, doubly, or trebly.

A cottise is a very narrow repetition of the charge following the outline, but with a narrow intervening space through which the field appears (Fig. 89).

When we come to the disposition of charges — the fore-going or any others —upon a field one very important rule

Fig 89.

must be observed. Of course there are a few exceptions, as there are to most other rules, but there are very few indeed.

The rule is that colour must not be placed upon colour, nor metal upon metal. The rule does not apply to furs, for one fur may be placed upon another, and either colour or metal may be placed on fur, or *vice versa*. So that if the field be metal, the charge must be of colour or fur.

But if the field be partly of colour and metal, a charge which is super-imposed over both may correctly be of either.

The rule does not apply to bordures, and does not apply to a crest.

CHAPTER XII

CHARGES—HERALDIC ANIMALS, ETC.

An enumeration of the various objects which in some coat of arms or another make their appearance would be quite out of place in a work of the size of the present one. I propose, therefore, only to deal with a few which are almost exclusively heraldic in their use. Chief amongst these is the lion. The relationship of the heraldic variety to the natural animal is becoming a matter of uncertainty.

Fig. 90.

So long as the intention is apparent, one may draw a heraldic lion as one pleases, subject to a due conformity to the laws of the science as to its position. A lion, like any other animal or object used in heraldry, may be of any heraldic tincture, or it may be " proper," *i.e.* represented in its natural colour.

The chief positions known to heraldry for

Fig. 91.

Fig. 92.

its animals are best exemplified by the lion, and are as follows :—

> Rampant (Fig. 90).
> Passant (Fig. 91).
> Statant (Fig. 92).
> Sejant (Fig. 93).
> Sejant-erect (Fig. 94).
> Couchant (Fig. 95).
> Dormant (Fig. 96).
> Saliant (Fig. 97).

Then the position of the head must be added to these terms, save it be in profile. A lion full-faced is guardant (Fig. 98), but if the head be turned to look to the back, it is regardant (Fig. 99).

Thus the lions in the arms of England are

Fig. 93.

Fig. 94.

Fig. 95.

Fig. 96.

passant guardant, whilst the lion in the coat of Scotland is simply rampant.

Although some of these positions in actual practice will only be met with in the case of the lion, the terms, nevertheless, are supposed

to apply to all other animals with a few
exceptions, chief amongst which are the following. A griffin when in the
rampant position is termed
"segreant"; a stag passant
is termed "trippant," and a
stag, horse, or dog extended
at full speed is termed
"courant." A stag standing
still with its head turned to
the spectator is said to be
"at gaze."

Parts of animals con-
stantly occur. Thus the upper half of a lion is

FIG. 97.

a "demi-lion," the head and neck is termed "a
lion's head," the paw
is a "jamb." But
whenever a part of

FIG. 98.

FIG. 99.

an animal or anything else occurs, it is either
"couped," *i.e.* cut with a clean line, or
"erased" (Fig. 4), that is, torn in a jagged line.

I

FIG. 100.

FIG 101.

VIRTUS · IN · ARDUIS

FIG. 102.

FIG. 103.

TOUT · JOUR · PRÊT

The distinction must always be made, save that a crest is presumed to be couped unless specified to be erased.

The head of an animal, if cut off close behind the ears leaving no part of the neck visible and repre- sented *affrontée*, is termed "caboshed" (Fig. 100), but a lion's or leopard's head in this caboshed form is termed its "face" (Fig. 101), and then the use of the term caboshed is unneces- sary. The head of a fox if caboshed is termed a "mask."

The curiosities which heraldry has invented in the way of animals are legion. The most important, however, are the dra- gon (with four legs,

FIG. 104.

Fig. 102), the wyvern (with two, Fig. 103), the griffin (the head and wings and legs of an eagle joined to the body, hind legs and tail of a lion, Fig. 104), the unicorn (too familiar to need description, Fig. 105), and the "heraldic tyger." This has a head something like a wolf with the body and tail of a lion.

The heraldic antelope is another curious creature (Fig. 106).

Heraldry has assigned wings to almost every existing creature. The pegasus or winged horse is not exclusively heraldic, but winged bulls and winged stags, for example, are occasionally met with.

Other animals have scales and fins and webbed feet and a fish tail supplied;

FIG. 105.   Fig. 106.

and we then have a series which, commencing with the merman and mermaid, supplies also the sea-lion and sea-wolf. The sea-dog (Fig. 107), I fancy, is really a beaver.

Birds, of course, play an important part in armory, and chief amongst them is the eagle, which is usually found "displayed" (Figs. 108 and 109), and when in this position it is frequently double-headed.

Fig. 107.

Fig. 108.

Fig. 109.

Fig. 110.

This position is confined to the eagle, the alerion, and possibly the hawk. Other positions are "close," "volant," "rising." The latter term has been officially applied to every position of the wings save close and volant. Personally, I prefer, therefore, always to supplement it by stating a bird to be rising "with wings displayed," or "with wings elevated and addorsed," or "with wings addorsed and inverted," or "with wings displayed and inverted."

Heraldry has not been so prolific in its invention of birds as of animals. The martlet is exclusively heraldic (Fig. 110), and is a swallow (martin) without feet. Most text-books say also that it has no beak, but, as a matter of fact, it is always drawn with one. An alerion, on the other hand, is not drawn with either beak or feet, being an eagle displayed, minus such adjuncts.

The heraldic pelican, however, is nothing like the real bird, but is usually depicted much the same as an eagle. It is usually found pecking its breast and with drops of blood issuing therefrom, when it is said to be "vulning" (*i.e.* wounding) itself. It is very frequently depicted standing in its nest, with young therein feeding on the drops of blood which are falling. The bird is then said to be "in her piety" (Fig. 111).

All birds of prey when described as "armed" of such a colour have the beak and claws so represented, and the term "armed" is similarly applied to the griffin. When used for a lion it refers to its claws, and for a bull, or goat, or ram it relates to the animal's horns. A stag, however, is "attired." "Langued,"

FORTI ET FIDELI NIHIL DIFFICILE

FIG. 111.   FIG. 112.

of course, refers to the tongue, and "unguled" to the hoofs.

A peacock with its tail displayed is called "a peacock in his pride" (Fig. 112), and the term is also applied to a turkey-cock.

A hawk is always belled on one or both legs, and may then be belled of a specified colour. If "belled and jessed," the thongs by which the bells are attached are also of the same colour.

A cock may be "combed, wattled, and jelloped" of a different colour.

Fish do not play a very important part in heraldry, but they have two terms peculiar to themselves, viz. "hauriant" and "naiant." The latter, of course, indicates the horizontal position of swimming, whilst "hauriant" indicates that the creature is erect, though it is necessary to state whether the head be up or down. A dolphin is often met with, and when naiant is also usually "embowed," *i.e.* bent.

Trees, fruit, and flowers are constantly occurring, but need little explanation as to the terms employed, save that the trunk of a tree is often "eradicated," when the root must be shown. A sheaf of wheat is termed a "garb," and fruit and flowers alike may be "slipped and leaved," or the contrary. The heraldic rose (Fig. 5) is represented without stalk or leaves unless these are specified. The trefoil, quatrefoil, and cinquefoil are simply conventionalised leaves, but whilst the trefoil is always shown with a stalk, the quatrefoil and cinquefoil are not unless so blazoned.

The fleur-de-lis has been the subject of much controversy, but is now usually considered a conventional form of the iris.

There is scarcely an object under the sun

which at some time or another has not been
introduced in a coat of arms, as may be gathered
from the assertion that the following can all be
found in genuine arms, viz. St. John's head in
a charger, a locomotive (Fig. 113), a woman's
breast distilling milk, a sausage on a grid-iron,

FIG. 113.　　　　FIG. 114.

Noah's ark, a safety-lamp, a 40-feet telescope,
a radiometer (Fig. 114), and a corrugated boiler
flue. Consequently, it is hopeless to attempt
anything in the nature of a list. I must therefore confine my remaining remarks to one or
two minor objects which are peculiarly heraldic
or have special terms in use regarding them.
The sun is always spoken of as "in his

splendour "; a mullet (Fig. 56 c) is a star which if pierced should be so described. It is of five points, unless a greater number are specified, but a star with wavy rays is an estoile. A (cockle) shell is an "escallop." When a cross has its ends cut short ("coupled"), these being crossed by other limbs, it is termed a cross-crosslet. There are over a hundred heraldic varieties of the cross; the most important of which are the crosses flory (Fig. 19), patée (Fig. 114), botonny (Fig. 19), moline, and potent.

The roundle, *i.e.* a plain circular disc of colour, has various names belonging to it, being termed a "bezant" when gold, a "plate" when silver, a "torteau" when red, a "hurt" when azure, a "pomeis" when green, a "golpe" when purple, and a "pellet" or "ogress" when black, but if composed of horizontal wavy bars alternately argent and azure, it is termed "a fountain" (Fig. 16). A ring, it may be remarked, is termed an annulet.

INDEX

117

THE END